The Modern West

Bassim Hamadeh, CEO and Publisher
Jennifer Codner, Senior Field Acquisitions Editor
Michelle Piehl, Senior Project Editor
Abbey Hastings, Associate Production Editor
Jess Estrella, Senior Graphic Designer
Stephanie Kohl, Licensing Associate
Jennifer Redding, Interior Designer
Natalie Piccotti, Director of Marketing
Kassie Graves, Vice President of Editorial
Jamie Giganti, Director of Academic Publishing

Cover image copyright © Depositphotos/sepavone.

Printed in the United States of America.

ISBN: 978-1-5165-1722-0 (pbk) / 978-1-5165-1723-7 (br) / 978-1-5165-4715-9 (al)

The Modern West

Issues and Perspectives

First Edition

Edited by Scott Lingenfelter

Grand Valley State University

For Andrew—keep laughing and singing

Contents

Introduction

Objectives

- Analyze eight issues central to the rise of the West to global power after 1500
- Assess recent perspectives on these eight crucial issues
- Develop eight skills essential for 21st century professionals

History classes are great at delivering content. Every history teacher worth his or her salt labors over learning activities that help you understand what happened in the past. This is done with the best of intentions and comes with the sincere belief that knowing the past helps us make the most of living in the present.

What's harder to do, but more essential I believe, is to create a class environment that challenges you to develop skills that you can use in the future. That's what this book aims to do. Think of it as an easy-to-read learning companion that gives you a chance to develop eight skills that will be a real asset to you. We'll do that by analyzing eight issues central to the major storyline in modern history: how did the West rise to global power after 1500 and what did that mean for the rest of the world? Since much of our global story is still to be written, we're talking about the future here—and *you* are that future. That should change the way you look at the past.

This collection includes topics on the academy's radar, like the media, cities, the environment, the lived experience of war, and ideology and power, but bare bones, the book's contents (roughly chronological) look something like this:

Issues	Skills
Media & the Masses	Contextualizing People and Events
Migrations & Encounters	Seeing Patterns of Continuity and Change
Cities & Revolution	Making the Most of Comparisons
Industry & Poverty	Reasoning Chronologically
War & the Environment	Understanding Causation
Individuals & History	Interpreting Sources
Ideology & Power	Developing a Persuasive Argument
Violence & the Body Politic	Doing Digital Research

PART I

I N THE FIRST FOUR CHAPTERS, we will examine a cluster of movements that set the modern West on course to become the preeminent global region. Those movements—the Renaissance and Reformation, the Scientific Revolution, the Enlightenment, the Atlantic revolutions, and industrialization—together made for epoch-making dynamism. We will take a closer look at them here through the lens of four issues that open a revealing window on the West. Those issues are media and the masses, migrations and encounters, cities and revolution, and industry and poverty.

2

Chapter 1

Chapter Skill	Contextualizing People and Events
Chapter Issue	Media & the Masses
Chapter Objectives (Students will...)	• Identify three specific ways in which new media shaped the Reformation Era • Analyze one current perspective on the relationship between the media and the Reformation • Demonstrate in a discussion on the media and the Reformation the ability to contextualize people and events
Assignments and Assessments	1. Read the Setup Narrative 2. Listen to the Lecture(s) 3. Read the Perspectives excerpt 4. Take part in a role-playing Class Discussion

Setup Narrative: Media & the Masses

Few events affected the modern West more than the Protestant Reformation, and few things held the key to the Reformation like the printing press. Within a century of Martin Luther's clash with the Catholic Church hierarchy, Europe was a very different place. Masses of people followed this acrimonious theological debate and its ripple effect at a time when religion was a vital state matter—and one of life or death if you were labeled a heretic. Gutenberg's press also set in motion a major chain reaction. Printed material proliferated and with it literacy, and then with literacy new notions of conscience. All told, the result was a truly powerful cluster of changes.

"Here I stand. I can do no other." With these words, Martin Luther ushered in a new age of Western history. Here we stand five hundred years later and we can see that what he said at the Diet of Worms in 1521 tells quite a story, one that goes far beyond an arid religious controversy. First, it's a story about how people responded to a crisis in late medieval Catholicism. There were several responses to the problems of corruption, clerical wealth, and papal political ambitions. Luther's was one of many. He and other protesters akin to him (hence *Protestants*) focused on three basic ideas, sometimes called the Three Solas because of the first Latin word in each expression: *sola scriptura* (by Biblical authority alone), *sola fide* (by faith alone), and *sola gratia* (by grace alone). Sometimes a couple more are added: *solo Christo* (by Christ alone) and *soli Deo gloria* (glory to God alone). In time, their break from the Catholic Church, easily the most important institution in the Middle Ages, fragmented Western Christianity into a number of major denominations and smaller splinter groups. However, what was apparently a church clash became a movement with far deeper roots.

The Reformation—which is a movement in two parts, the Protestant reforms and the Catholic Counter-Reformation—stood on the shoulders of the gains of the Renaissance, that marvelous rebirth of classical learning and virtues that we associate with the great books and art that appeared at the dawn of modern history. The trenchant intelligence of Petrarch and Erasmus, the frescoes of Masaccio, the dome of Brunelleschi, the sculptures and chapel ceiling of Michel-angelo, and the innovations of Leonardo da Vinci owed their work to a new climate around the Mediterranean after the agony of the Black Death. In this rebirth after widespread death, a renewed emphasis on several "-isms" transformed the modern West. Secularism, individualism, realism, and activism were now as sacred to human fulfillment as mass and the sacraments had been to Catholics for generations. And this became a movement, among a tiny elite at first, but then in time, far beyond.

That movement altered the benchmarks of the late medieval world, including the need to take a long, hard look at Catholic Church doctrine and practice. The Protestant reformers would have remained a small, if determined, little clutch if not for three things. First, these reformers were organizers and they established new confessions (Lutherans, Presbyterians, etc.) that took root across Europe. Second, kings and other princes used this gathering reform movement to do something they had been itching to do for a long time: break free from the power of the popes of Rome. They appealed to righteous means to accomplish what were often quite unholy ends. Third, the masses of commoners across Europe were attracted to these new ideas about church and calling because they could serve as tools for social, as well as religious, protest. And they made good use of them—though not always successfully. But taken together, even this movement would not have been possible without a single invention: the printing press.

The first printing press with movable type was (not surprisingly) of Chinese origin in the 11th century, but Gutenberg's timing was perfect. His press came in the middle of the 15th century just on the cusp of the Age of Discovery, the Reformation, and the Scientific Revolu-tion, none of which were conceivable without the press. That press freed information from oral constraints and made literacy a priority for the masses (as well as the spectacles to see the new print). When people read, they can think for themselves, and when people of the time thought for themselves they began to discover the significance of one of the defining aspects of what we call "modern"—the individual's conscience. That conscience would be sorely needed as not everything that appeared in print was credible and reliable.

Lecture
Pay attention to the chapter lecture(s), either online or in class.

Tips on Contextualizing People and Events

- Remember that each age is its own ecosystem. We can't expect a medieval traveler on the Canterbury Trail to have used GPS.
- Study the times thoroughly enough that you are comfortable describing people and events in their natural web of connections and relationships. In this chapter, that means getting familiar with the reach of the print media in 16th century Europe.
- Draw conclusions about people of a given time based on what *they* could see at the time. We know what happened a century later, but they couldn't.

The Case Against a "Print Revolution"

by Mark Knights and Angela McShane

Reluctant to place so much emphasis on one new technology, some scholars perceive a wider early modern communications revolution (Behringer 2006). An item of print only had impact once it was disseminated and that relied on improvements in marketing but even more fundamentally in the means of transport. Over the early modern period space and time shrank, as better roads, ships, canals and postal services improved communications. The Habsburgs developed a postal system in the early sixteenth century; and by the end of the eighteenth century there were about 2,500 postal stations in Germany and France. Travelling time between towns was cut dramatically. Thus, whereas in 1500 it took thirty days to go from Hamburg to Augsburg, by 1800 this had been cut to just five for postal couriers (Behringer 2006, 364). News—both manuscript newsletters and then printed newspapers—flowed along such routes; indeed, it depended on them. Without these developments in transport infrastructure the impact of the 'print revolution' might have been rather more restricted.

Historians have also argued that the revolution from a hand-written (scribal) and oral culture to a print culture has been exaggerated (Crick and Walsham 2004, 'Introduction'). Workshops of late medieval scribes had already created large numbers of books and manuscripts that proliferated across Europe. Indeed, whereas for Simplicissimus the character of print shaped the way he wrote, scribal practices and styles could in turn influence print which aped letter forms or imitated manuscript formats. Nor was scribal production suddenly replaced by printing. Hand-written copies of texts continued to flourish at least until the late seventeenth century, especially where censorship restricted the activities of authors and publishers. For much of the early modern period a literate, rather than a print, culture was what mattered, with a key divide between those who possessed or had access to texts and could read them, and those who did not.

Mark Knights and Angela McShane, "From Pen to Print - A Revolution in Communications?," *The European World 1500-1800: An Introduction to Early Modern History*, ed. Beat Kümin, pp. 189-193. Copyright © 2009 by Taylor & Francis Group. Reprinted with permission.

Just as scribal practices remained vibrant, oral culture was not undermined or even replaced by 'print culture' ('Popular Culture(s)' in Part IV). Rather, print and oral culture existed in mutually reinforcing and stimulating ways: what was talked about found its way into print, and what was printed was talked about. Indeed, periodicals aimed at the middling sort—such as the Tatler—appeared with the specific intention of providing men and women in taverns, markets, clubs, salons and coffee houses with topics of conversation, and learned journals like the Royal Society's *Philosophical Transactions* stimulated debates all over Europe.

The case for a print revolution argues that it was instrumental in spreading knowledge and information. Yet it can be argued that print spread disinformation. Contemporaries used print but they also distrusted it. This was less the case in the scientific and cultural worlds but more so in the religious, political, social and economic arenas. Far from verifying and establishing 'truth' and 'reason', print could be used to distort and invert them. Paradoxically, then, although print 'fixed' texts, it could unfix truth. Indeed, partisans of all stripes believed their rivals engaged in deliberate attempts to mislead readers. In those circumstances, traditional forms of gauging credit—for example, through social or religious status—remained highly important. Distrust was further boosted by the ubiquitous anonymity of the medium—almost half the number of titles had no attributed author—which apparently allowed writers to lie without fear of reprisal (Figure 1.1). The developing nature of the book trade also encouraged the more disreputable end of the trade, especially in France and England, where by the eighteenth century a 'grub street' of impoverished authors, printers and publishers readily invented stories or took both sides of an argument in order to stoke the public appetite. As Filippo di Strata put it: 'The pen is a virgin, the printing press a whore' (Brooks 2005, 4). Print was a business, like any other, that pandered to markets. The profits were as much financial as cultural or intellectual.

Nor, it could be argued, was the print revolution necessarily one that undermined the Ancien Régime; indeed, it could even support

FIGURE 1.1 This anti-cavalier broadside ballad was published, probably with parliamentary approval, in 1642 at the outset of the English Civil War and as part of the enormous printed propaganda campaigns that broke out from 1640. An attack on the pillaging behaviour of cavalier soldiers, copies could be sent all over the country by post and they could be pasted onto whipping posts in market-places, on church doors and on the walls in alehouses—in any place where both cavaliers and roundheads could see them. Anon., *The English Irish Soldier* (1642): British Library, London.

and strengthen the role of authoritarian governments. The type of print products available remained surprisingly traditional. Theological debate kept a high profile in the output of the eighteenth century, for all the so-called secularizing tendency of the Enlightenment. Printed satire may have helped to delegitimize notions of a sacred monarchy or an unquestioned Church, but religious texts, sermons, schoolbooks, proclamations and government apologists served to defend it. And print could enhance and enforce authority within the state. Bureaucratization, centralization, more effective fiscal powers, militarization and the defence of ideologies of order were all facilitated by better communications. Moreover, the financial revolutions of the eighteenth century, which saw large amounts of private money invested in governmental debts and loans, relied to an important extent on information being available to investors via the newspapers and other forms of print. Indeed, the activities of the state stimulated printed news: the 'coranto', an early form of newspaper, which developed at the beginning of the seventeenth century in the Netherlands, from an earlier French example, concentrated entirely on foreign affairs and European conflicts.

Finally, even if there was a print revolution in the sense of the greater production and availability of the press, it is hard to establish a clear correlation between text and action. Because propaganda was available, does that guarantee that its message would be followed? Was the French Revolution the result of the Enlightenment and the Enlightenment the result of the press?

ASSESSMENT

It is certain that distribution and accessibility of texts increased Europe-wide from the fifteenth century onwards. Historians and literary scholars have pointed to revolutions not just in reading habits and print formats but also in religion, science, politics and wider cultural belief-systems that seem attributable to the press. Yet how far they actually were remains hotly contested. On the one hand, there are many who see the press as really instrumental in fostering a religion of the word, such as Protestantism; as disseminating ideas that both spread a rebirth of classicism and undermined the established order; and as contributing to the state and national identity as well as to a culture of entertainment and new forms of writing. On the other hand, there are scholars who stress that print did not provoke a radical break with the past and that its impact was often dependent on other technologies, especially transport. Far from undercutting an oral and literate culture, print merely reinvigorated it in different ways; print was not always available, especially among the poor and less well-off; print did not fix truth and reason but promulgated lies, propaganda and polemical irrationalities as one author railed against another. Moreover, the correlation between text and behaviour is uncertain.

Yet these are not mutually exclusive interpretations. We might simply want to build important caveats into our analysis of the transformative power of print. Indeed, in this respect it is helpful to think of the ways in which modern digital technologies coexist with older ones, are taken up at different rates with varying degrees of enthusiasm and foster new ways of thinking and behaving. When we evaluate such questions we are thrown back to problems faced by those who lived in the early modern period. Do changes in communicative practices change the way we think and what we say? Should we embrace transforming technologies or be sceptical about them or both? Are there justifiable limits on the freedom of expression or publishing copyright? How do we discern lies and misinformation, and what can we do about them? These are early modern questions that have a twenty-first-century urgency.

Discussion themes

1. Is the term 'print revolution' misleading?

2. Did changes in communicative practices change belief and behaviour in early modern Europe?

3. Was print necessarily subversive of authority?

Bibliography

(A) Sources

Bacon, Francis (1620), *The New Organon: Or True Directions Concerning the Interpretation of Nature,* London

Grimmelshausen, Johan Jacob (1989), *Simplicissimus* [1668/9], trans. S. Goodrich, Sawtry

(B) Literature

Anderson, Benedict (1983), *Imagined Communities: Reflections on the Origin and Spread of Nationalism,* London

Behringer, Wolfgang ed. (2006), 'Communication in Historiography', special issue of *German History,* 24:3

Blanning, T. C. W. (2002), *The Culture of Power and the Power of Culture: Old Regime Europe* 1660–1789, Oxford

Brooks, Douglas A. ed. (2005), *Printing and Parenting in Early Modern England,* Aldershot

Cressy, David (1980), *Literacy and the Social Order: Reading and Writing in Tudor and Stuart England,* Cambridge

Crick, Julia and Walsham, Alexandra eds (2004), *The Uses of Script and Print, 1300–1700,* Cambridge

Darnton, Robert (1995), *The Forbidden Best-Sellers of Pre-Revolutionary France,* London

* Eisenstein, Elizabeth L. (1979), *The Printing Press as an Agent of Change: Communications and Cultural Transformations in Early Modern Europe,* 2 vols, Cambridge

Ginzburg, Carlo (1980), *The Cheese and the Worms: The Cosmos of a Sixteenth-Century Miller,* Baltimore, Md.

* Grafton, Anthony, Eisenstein, Elizabeth L. and Johns, Adrian (2002), 'AHR Forum: How Revolutionary was the Print Revolution', *American Historical Review* 107, 84–128

Houston, R. A. (2002), *Literacy in Early Modern Europe,* 2nd edn, London

Pettegree, Andrew (2002), 'Printing and the Reformation', in: The Beginnings of *English Protestantism,* ed. P. Marshall and A. Ryrie, Cambridge

Raven, James, Small, Helen and Tadmor, Naomi eds (1996), *The Practice and Representation of Reading in England,* Cambridge

Scribner, Robert (1981), *For the Sake of Simple Folk: Popular Propaganda for the German Reformation,* London.

Sharpe, Kevin (2000), *Reading Revolutions: The Politics of Reading in Early Modern England,* New Haven, Conn.

Zaret, David (2000), *Origins of Democratic Culture: Printing, Petitions and the Public Sphere in Early Modern England,* Princeton, NJ.

(C) Web Resources

'English Broadside Ballad Archive', University of California, Santa Barbara: <http://www.english.ucsb.edu/emc/ballad_project/>

'The Gutenberg Bible' (*c.* 1454), British Library: <http://prodigi.bl.uk/gutenbg/file1.htm#top>

'Index Librorum Prohibitorum' (1557–), IHSP: <http://www.fordham.edu/halsall/mod/indexlibrorum.html>

'John Foxe's *Book of Martyrs',* Humanities Research Institute, Sheffield: <http://www.hrionline.ac.uk/johnfoxe/>

'Stephen Fry and the Gutenberg Press', BBC 4 programme in 'The Medieval Season': <http://www.bbc.co.uk/bbcfour/medieval/gutenberg.shtml>

Questions for Reflection

The print revolution transformed the media landscape of early modern Europe—or did it? In this Perspectives excerpt, the authors question common assumptions about a "print revolution" and its impact on the Reformation and much else besides. As you reflect on the impact of media, then and now, answer the following questions.

1. What are the common assumptions about a "print revolution"? How is it often used to tell the story of the Reformation?

2. Who were the Habsburgs? What is their connection to the Protestant Reformation?

3. According to the authors, the print revolution would not have been possible without other things to support it. Like what? Do you agree?

4. What do you think Filippo di Strata meant by "The pen is a virgin, the printing press a whore"?

5. What do the authors mean by "...although print 'fixed' texts, it could unfix truth."? What's a good example of this?

6. According to this excerpt, what changed with the advent of the printing press and what did not?

7. Do you think the point of the excerpt is that there was no print revolution or that something more, something bigger was happening? How does this help us place people and events in the context of the time?

8. After answering the questions above, what to you is still a puzzle about the media, the masses, and the Reformation?

Activities Menu

Your instructor may assign one or more of the following learning activities:

Prewriting Exercise

Take a minute and write a paragraph (half page of notebook paper) on what you know about the major problems in the Catholic Church around 1500. Be honest!

Media

Select a relevant video program from any of the following and write a one-page (double-spaced) reaction.

+ TED Talk
+ Munk Debates
+ C-SPAN
+ Crash Course

Source Search

Select and read two related primary sources found online at the Modern History Sourcebook and incorporate them into your discussion.

Class Discussion I

Use the eight questions above as the basis of a class discussion. Write out your answers ahead of time so that you will have something to say.

Class Discussion II

Use the questions above to talk about the parallels between the print revolution of the 16th century and the ongoing digital revolution today. Are there similarities? If so, what are they? Is "fake news" common to both? How so? Can this be overcome?

Role-Playing Exercise

Divide the class into Protestant and Catholic "teams." Have a couple of students represent each side's perspective on the value of the new media of the age. What was good about them? What was not so good?

Suggested Reading

Elizabeth Eisenstein, *The Printing Revolution in Early Modern Europe* (2005)

Mark Knights and Angela McShane, "From Pen to Print—A Revolution in Communications?" in *The European World, 1500–1800: An Introduction to Early Modern History* (2009)

Diarmaid MacCulloch, *The Reformation: A History* (2005)

Giuseppe Mazzotta, *Cosmopiesis: The Renaissance Experiment* (2001)

Merry Weisner-Hanks, *The Renaissance and Reformation: A History in Documents* (2011)

Chapter 2

Chapter Skill	Seeing Patterns of Continuity and Change
Chapter Issue	Migrations & Encounters
Chapter Objectives (Students will...)	• Identify three specific ways in which global migrations and cross-cultural encounters shaped the early modern world • Assess current perspectives on the transatlantic slave trade and the growth of London illustrating the impact of early modern migrations and encounters • Demonstrate in a short essay on migrations and encounters the ability to see patterns of continuity and change over time
Assignments and Assessments	1. Read the Setup Narrative 2. Listen to the Lecture(s) 3. Read the Perspectives excerpts 4. Compose a three-page Essay in answer to the assigned prompt 5. Take a brief "check-up" Quiz

Setup Narrative: Migrations & Encounters

In Chapter 1, we examined an intellectual and institutional movement. In this chapter, we look at another kind of movement and mobility: physical and social. The age of European exploration and discovery left the Atlantic world permanently changed. The exchange of people, animals, goods, and food—often called the Columbian Exchange—tied Europe, Africa, and the Americas together in unprecedented ways. The transatlantic slave trade did the same, but now people were the commodities, and human trafficking became a persistent thread in the story of the West. Both involved voluntary and involuntary migrations and both included fascinatingly complex cultural encounters.

This was an era of adventure. Think of it: Sailing across treacherous seas to exotic lands in search of untold riches in the name of a powerful king or queen and their admiring court; or the chance to escape trouble at home by enjoying the life of a soldier of fortune abroad; or the opportunity to discover an unimaginable array of vibrant flora and fauna in the name of the new science; or a vision of salvation that was worthy of real sacrifice. From a welter of mixed motives, Europe expanded beyond the intellectual horizons of the Renaissance and Reformation to new geographical horizons that beckoned. The Portuguese set up trading colonies in the Indian Ocean, and the Dutch seized the coveted Spice Islands farther to the east. The Spanish subdued Native American empires. The French concentrated on the lucrative sugar colonies of the Caribbean, while the British decided to settle people of all ranks with the promise of land to the north. Fortunes were made, families took root in new places, and familiar ways and customs were abandoned for the chance at a fresh start.

But, of course, people had called these "new" places home for eons. Indian Ocean ports had been the dynamic reserve of Chinese and African traders for centuries. The islands of the South Pacific were peopled with a mélange of East and South Asian seafaring survivors who thought of more than spices when they fought tribal rivals for home turf. Until decimated by disease and warfare, the Carib peoples dominated the life and culture of Middle America, as did scores of native nations in North America on the soil of what one day would be one nation of nearly equal diversity. All of this meant an unprecedented number of encounters that would transform the Atlantic world. Some of the encounters were peaceful, many were not. Nearly all of them meant looking at native peoples through ethnic stereotypes that hardened into racial prejudices. And, let's face it, sometimes all for a buck.

To put it in the practical vernacular of the time, the loss of native peoples, sometimes called the Great Dying, left Europeans with a labor shortage. This they filled with millions of West Africans, targeted and captured to work the first globalized economic enterprises. They were caught up in the Triangular Trade of the Atlantic and suffered the horrific voyage called the Middle Passage of that triangle. Most ended up passing short and surreal lives on Caribbean plantations or in Brazilian mines, but many were transported to North America to toil on cotton and rice plantations. Their lives and labor became part of a broader new economy of merchant capitalism funded by new banks and joint-stock ventures, the likes of which the world had never seen, especially when considering that the market capitalization of the Dutch East India Company still dwarfs today's behemoths like Apple and Microsoft.

The economic and racial legacies of this era resonate troublingly, not least because the nations of Europe and America were preaching enlightened popular sovereignty and inherent personal rights at the very moment the slave trade reached its peak (between 1776 and 1780). How was that possible? And there is another critical aspect here: How were African societies affected by the transatlantic slave trade? That is the focus of the most recent research and of one of the excerpts below.

Lecture
Pay attention to the chapter lecture(s), either online or in class.

Tips on Seeing Patterns of Continuity and Change

+ Remember that much of our existence is interpreted through the lens of what's the same and what's different. That's a skill. The most innovative among us sense a "discontinuity," a major change, around the corner.

+ Study an era closely so that you begin to see patterns in what's keeping societies static and what's shaking them up. In this chapter, that means getting to know how and why London is a portrait of the age.

+ Draw conclusions about an era appreciating the fact that old and new often sit side by side, and that major changes are not always obvious to contemporaries.

The First Stage of the Impact of World Trade on Tropical Africa: The Export Slave Trade

by J.D. Fage and William Tordoff

The demand for slaves derived, of course, from the vast expansion of the labour-intensive plantations which Europeans had developed in the Americas. The New World surpassed Europe and the Atlantic and Gulf of Guinea islands as a market for African slaves in the third quarter of the sixteenth century. But its absorption of African labour remained relatively small until the Iberian monopoly of its exploitation was broken by the actions of the Dutch West India Company in the second quarter of the seventeenth century. From then on, the numbers of African slaves taken to the Americas grew steadily up to about the 1790s, when the French Revolutionary and Napoleonic Wars began to disrupt traffic across the Atlantic. After the restoration of peace in 1815, the Atlantic slave trade began to revive. But Europeans had now begun actively to question the morality of trading in men, and since at the same time their more prospering economies had reached a stage when investment in slaves seemed less remunerative than investment in other means of production, measures began to be taken to outlaw the slave trade. During the 1830s, these began to have some effect north of the equator. One consequence of this was for the volume of trade south of the equator to increase, but by the end of the 1860s the whole Atlantic trade was coming to a close, the ultimately determinant factor being the abolition of slavery in the Americas.

When looking back at the Atlantic slave trade, historians and others were for long accustomed to think that the number of African slaves taken to the Americas must have amounted to at least 15 millions, and that it could well have been appreciably greater. Thus in 1936, R. R. Kuczynski, one of the first modern demographers to apply himself to African data, regarded 15 millions as 'rather a conservative figure'. But in the 1960s, Professor Philip D. Curtin realized that this commonly accepted figure of at least 15 millions derived merely from estimates made in 1861 by an American publicist; later writers had taken it up without inquiring into its authenticity. Curtin therefore set himself to survey as much of the literature relating to the import of slaves into the Americas, or their export westwards from Africa, as was necessary to establish reasonably reliable estimates for all the various regions and periods of the trade. Where he could find no consensus for the volume of a particular aspect of the trade, or where there was a gap in a series of published figures, he constructed new estimates which seemed to him best to fit the particular circumstances. In this way he arrived at an estimated grand total for the number of African slaves imported into the Americas of only 9,566,000.

The limitations of the exercise undertaken by Curtin are well set out in the preface to the book in which his work was published. He thought he would have done well if his figures were within plus or minus 20 per cent of the reality; elsewhere he wrote 'it is extremely unlikely that the ultimate total will turn out to be less than 8,000,000 or more than 10,500,000'. However his book served to inspire other historians to search among archives for runs of first-hand figures showing the volume of the Atlantic slave trade in particular places at particular times, and some of these historians, coming upon data which do not match with Curtin's figures, have been extremely critical of them. But this is to mistake his purpose, which was simply to get a better idea of the volume of the Atlantic slave trade, both in total and in its various aspects and phases, than the almost totally unsubstantiated estimates that had previously been uncritically accepted by scholars (including the present writer) who ought to have known better. In this, Curtin certainly succeeded. Over nearly two decades, the work of many 'dig-deepers' has demonstrated that some of his figures may have been too small, but overall his underestimates have been balanced by other figures that seem to have been too high. The result of the work done since the publication of Curtin's book—which in 1982 was conveniently summarized and interpreted by Professor Paul E. Lovejoy—has been to provide revised estimates which in grand total arrive at much the same result as that produced by Curtin. The main trends of the trade as discerned in 1982 are set out in Table 2.1.

TABLE 2.1   Estimated numbers of African slaves landed overseas by European traders

	To Old World Destinations		To the Americas		
	Totals	Annual Average	Totals	Annual Average	Totals
1451–1525	76,000	1,000			
1526–50	31,300	1,200	12,500	500	
1551–75	26,300	1,000	34,700	1,400	
1576–1600	16,300	600	96,000	3,800	293,000
1601–25	12,800	500	249,000	10,000	
1626–50	6,600	300	236,000	9,500	
1651–75	3,000	120	368,000	15,000	
1676–1700	2,700	100	616,000	25,000	1,494,000
1701–20			626,000	31,000	
1721–40			870,000	43,000	

1741–60		1,007,000	50,000	
1761–80		1,148,000	57,000	
1781–1800		1,561,000	78,000	5,212,000
1801–20		980,000	49,000	
1821–67		1,803,000	38,000	2,783,000
Totals	**175,000**	**9,607,000**		**9,782,000**

* The sources for this table are Philip D. Curtin, *The Atlantic Slave Trade: A Census (1969)*, especially his Tables 33 and 34, and Paul E. Lovejoy, 'The volume of the Atlantic slave trade: a synthesis', *Journal of African History*, vol. 23 (1982) pp. 473–501, especially his Tables 2–6. Lovejoy's book, *Transformations in Slavery: A History of Slavery in Africa* (1983), contains further information including, for example, estimates for the trans-Saharan, Red Sea and Indian Ocean export slave trades.

It must be emphasized that the figures in Table I are estimates for the numbers of Africans *landed overseas*, for the most part, of course, in the Americas. Such estimates are obviously relevant to the demographic history of the New World, but what those concerned with the history of African peoples want to know is how many men and women *left Africa*. Curtin worked primarily from figures for slaves landed overseas because he thought that by and large these were more reliable than those available for slaves shipped from Africa. Lovejoy accepted this up to 1700, but thereafter thought it feasible and better to use figures for slaves shipped from Africa. The figures given in Table I for the eighteenth and nineteenth centuries have therefore been calculated from Lovejoy's figures by allowing for an average loss of life en route of 15 per cent. The data available for these two centuries enables such an average to be calculated with some confidence. For earlier times, the loss of life at sea is likely to have been higher—though exactly how much higher is uncertain. But if the fairly conservative rate of loss of 20 per cent is assumed for times up to 1700, it is possible to suggest that the loss of people from Africa may have been of the order of the estimates given in Table 2.2.

TABLE 2.2 Estimated numbers of men and women taken from Africa by the Atlantic trade		
	Total Exported	**Annual Averages**
1451–1601	367,000	
1601–1700	1,867,000	19,000
1701–1800	6,133,000	61,000
1801–1867	3,274,000	33,000
Total	**11,641,000**	

This was undoubtedly one of the greatest population movements in history, and certainly the largest migration by sea before the great European emigration, also primarily to the Americas, which developed as the Atlantic slave trade was beginning to end. But it was not, of course, the only export of slaves from tropical Africa. For centuries Blacks had been taken northwards across the Sahara and down the Nile, and also across the Red Sea and the Indian Ocean. However, information on the numbers involved in these slave trades is nothing like as good as that for the Atlantic trade.

There is very little good quantitative data for the slave trade across the Sahara to North Africa. Such information as there is suggests that, although there is evidence of the presence of Blacks in North Africa in classical times, a systematic trans-Saharan slave trade on any scale probably did not develop until after the introduction of the camel and, more particularly, until after the Arab conquest of North Africa. The marching of men and women across a waterless desert must always have presented great problems, and prior to the ninth century it is thought unlikely that imports into North Africa can have averaged more than about 1,000 a year. However from about the ninth century onwards there is evidence for an organized trans-Saharan trade in slaves.* The exiguous data available suggests that it may have averaged something like 6,000 or 7,000 slaves a year until the 1880s (after which it was rapidly extinguished), though with peaks in the tenth and eleventh centuries at about 8,700 slave imports a year and in the first eighty years of the nineteenth century possibly as high as 14,500. Allowing for losses in transit and for slaves retained in Saharan societies, during the greater part of the period when the Atlantic trade was flourishing it is possible to suppose that an average of somewhere between 7,000 and 9,000 men and women a year could have been lost to Black Africa as a result of the trans-Saharan trade. A significantly greater rate of loss would have been incurred only in the first three-quarters of the nineteenth century (when the Atlantic trade was in decline). The trans-Saharan trade may therefore have in total removed from Black Africa almost as many people—some nine or ten millions—as did the Atlantic trade. If it be asked why such numbers appear to have made a much less obvious impact on the ethnic composition of the populations of North African and adjacent Near Eastern lands than was made on that of many American countries, it might be argued that a long-continuing infiltration of only a few thousand Blacks a year is unlikely to have led to such obvious results as the compression of the bulk of the Atlantic slave trade into little more than two recent centuries. Conversely it might be suggested that it would have been a good deal less damaging to the exporting populations in Black Africa. But more than numbers alone needs to be considered. While the slaves imported into the Americas were predominantly male, and efforts were commonly made to maintain a reservoir of black labour separate from white society, a large proportion of the slaves taken across the Sahara were female and were absorbed into the recipient populations as wives or concubines (and many of the younger males seem to have been converted into eunuchs). Therefore the Blacks taken across the Sahara would have been more easily assimilable than those taken to the Americas. In addition, the loss of potential wives and mothers would have made the demographic damage to Black African populations relatively greater than the numbers alone might suggest.

---

* The data that follow, for the Red Sea and Indian Ocean slave trades as well for that across the Sahara, are based on Ralph A. Austen, 'The trans-Saharan slave trade: a tentative census', in Henry A. Gemery & Jan S. Hogendorn (eds), *The uncommon market* (1979), pp. 23–76, as modified by tables 7.1 and 7.7 in Lovejoy's book.

The export of slaves by sea from the Red Sea and Indian Ocean coasts seems to have been like the Atlantic trade in that the major volume of the exports was apparently concentrated in a relatively short and recent period. The quantitative data available are no better than those available for the trans-Saharan trade. The best estimates available suggest that from about A.D. 800 to 1700, exports to the Near and Middle East and to western India might have averaged about 3,000 a year, with 2,000 going from the Red Sea coast and the remainder from the Indian Ocean coast. In the 1700S it seems likely that the two coasts may have shared equally in a slave trade averaging about 4,000 a year. It is generally agreed that the volume of the trade began to increase substantially from about the beginning of the nineteenth century, but there is argument as to the numbers that were actually exported. This is in large measure because a considerable but uncertain number of slaves brought down from the interior to the Indian Ocean coast were retained for employment on plantations in the coastlands and on the off-shore islands. The most reasonable estimate perhaps is that altogether something like 900,000 slaves may have been exported to Asian destinations in the nineteenth century, about half from the Red Sea coast and half from the Indian Ocean coast. By about the middle of the century, the growth was attracting the attention of the European interests that were then opposed to slave trading, with the result that increasingly effective measures were taken against it. The export of slaves from the Indian Ocean coast had virtually ceased by the 1870s, and by the 1890s the Red Sea trade had been reduced to a trickle.

The development of the Indian Ocean trade in the earlier nineteenth century coincides with a marked build-up of Omani power on the east coast which began towards the close of the previous century, and which culminated in 1840 in the removal of their major seat of government from Muscat to Zanzibar. With this, and backed with finance from Indian merchants resident at Zanzibar, there was associated a totally new development in which Arab-Swahili caravans went inland from the coast to the great lakes of East Africa and ultimately as far as the upper Congo. A principal cause of this seems to have been a growing European and Asian demand for ivory from East Africa, itself due in some measure to the demands of the rising European middle class for goods such as billiard balls and pianos, but also no doubt associated with the decline in exports of ivory from West Africa (which, via the European companies, had also traded with Asia, where African ivory was valued since it was better suited to carving than Asian ivory). But it is also clear that it was this new exploitation of trade routes from the east coast into the interior that made possible the great growth of the Indian Ocean slave trade from about 1800 onwards. Conversely, however, bearing in mind the previous absence of any such system of trade routes into the interior under the control of coastal merchants in the whole region between Somalia and the Zambezi, it is reasonable to conclude that the export of slaves from East Africa prior to 1800 was not on any very great scale. But for the first seventy or so years of the nineteenth century, exports of slaves from the Swahili coast seem likely to have averaged at least 6,000 slaves a year, and for the first ninety years exports across the Red Sea seem likely to have averaged at least 5,000 a year. In other words, for the greater part of the century slaves may have been exported to Asian destinations at the rate of at least 11,000 a year; some authorities would double this figure.

From the continental perspective, then, there would seem little question but that the significant period of the export slave trade in Africa runs from about the middle of the seventeenth century, when the Atlantic trade began to assume major dimensions, to about the middle of the nineteenth, after which the sea-borne slave trades were all rapidly extinguished. During this period of some 200 years, the evidence suggests that something like 14,000,000 men and women may have been taken out of Black Africa. The distribution through time would seem to have followed something like the following pattern:

TABLE 2.3 Estimated totals of slaves exported from Black Africa, c. 1650-C. 1870				
	Atlantic trade	Saharan trade	Indian Ocean and Red Sea trades	totals	annual average
1651–1700	1,230,000	350,000	150,000	1,730,000	35,000
1701–1750	2,350,000	350,000	200,000	2,900,000	58,000
1751–1800	3,780,000	350,000	200,000	4,330,000	87,000
1801–c. 1870	3,270,000	1,015,000	770,000	5,055,000	72,000
Totals	**10,630,000**	**2,065,000**	**1,320,000**	**14,015,000**	

The impact of these export trades obviously varied from one region of Black Africa to another. So far as the Atlantic trade was concerned, almost all the slaves were taken from the west coast, which was closest to the source of the demand in the Americas and was where Europeans had first established satisfactory trading relationships. It was only as the demand reached its peak towards the end of the eighteenth century, and when, in the nineteenth century, the measures taken against the Atlantic slave trade were initially concentrated north of the equator, that any significant numbers of slaves were taken by Europeans from eastern Africa—to the French plantations on the Mascarene islands as well as to America—and for these destinations together the total probably did not exceed 500,000. During the period of some 200 years when the export slave trades were at their height, West Africa north of the equator contributed something like 5,700,000 slaves to the Atlantic trade and must also have provided some proportion—possibly a half—of the 2,065,000 or so slaves exported across the Sahara. The other half would have been drawn from the eastern Sudan which, together with the Horn of Africa, would also have contributed something like 750,000 slaves to the Red Sea trade. South of the equator, Bantu Africa was divided between two slave-trading networks, feeding the Atlantic and the Indian Ocean systems respectively, the former taking about 4,550,000 slaves during these 200 years and the latter something like 750,000 (including slaves for the Mascarenes as well as for Asian lands, but excluding the substantial numbers retained for plantations on the east coast and its offshore islands).

While it is possible to construct broad estimates of the numbers of slaves exported between c. 1650 and c. 1870 from major regions such as the Sudan, West Africa or Bantu Africa, it is much more difficult to judge how each of such regions may have been affected by such a substantial depletion of its human resources. For one thing, we really have no idea how many other lives may have been lost in the business of securing slaves for export and in bringing them down to the coast. Such contemporary estimates as there are—for example the oft-quoted mid-nineteenth-century statement of David Livingstone that for every slave exported from east central Africa ten other human beings lost their lives—are hardly more than guesses. In Livingstone's case, it is reasonable to assume that his judgement was coloured both by the appalling scenes he had witnessed and by a compulsion to use his evidence to secure the maximum support for the European anti-slave trade campaign. It also needs to be appreciated that such estimates relate only to particular parts of Africa at particular points of time: in Livingstone's case it must be remembered that his travels were largely limited to the bands of territory within which the Arab-Swahili traders themselves moved. Neither the activities of these traders nor the overall environment in which they operated were necessarily typical of other regions or of other times. There can be no question but that weak or sick slaves could be killed or left to die along the trails that led to the coast, and that raids and wars were among the means used to secure slaves, thus occasioning further loss of life, whether directly, or indirectly through the destruction of crops, cattle and shelter or the spread of disease. But it is equally true that such destruction could result from natural disasters, such as drought or flood and pestilence, and that these natural disasters could also lead to slaves being provided for the trade—and to population fleeing to strengthen the resources of societies in more favourable environments (something which made it easier for them to acquire and trade in slaves).

It is frankly impossible to make any firm assessment of the total effect on Black Africa of the monstrous rape of its life, manpower and productivity by the export slave trades. Even the most elementary issue, namely the extent to which the export of slaves affected the size and growth of populations, cannot really be tackled, since usually nothing but the crudest estimates exist for the size of African populations, their rates of natural increase, or their geographical distribution for any period before the present century.

For what it is worth, demographers, basing themselves on current data, have supposed that in 1650, when the Atlantic slave trade really began to take off, the population of the whole continent may have been about 100,000,000, and that up to that time it may have been growing at the low rate of 0.12 or 0.11 per cent per annum. South of the Sahara, Black Africa is unlikely to have had more than four-fifths of the total population, so when the export slave trades began to reach their peak, the affected population would have been at most 80,000,000. An annual natural increase, i.e. an excess of birth over deaths, of 0.11 per cent, i.e. of about 88,000, would have been well above the 35,000 which has been suggested as the estimated mean annual loss due directly to the export slave trades in the second half of the seventeenth century. On the other hand, the estimated mean annual direct losses suggested for the second half of the eighteenth century and the first half of the nineteenth—87,000 and 72,000 respectively—seem to have been of the same order of magnitude as the estimated annual natural increase. Indeed, the demographers assume that during 1650–1800 the population of the continent as a whole remained static at around 100,000,000. By implication, therefore, they must also suppose that the indirect loss of life due to slave trading was fairly minimal.*

Of course the incidence of the export slave trades was not felt uniformly through sub-Saharan Africa. There was, for instance, the important difference—already indicated—between the trade conducted by Christian Europeans to the Americas and the Muslim-conducted trades to North African and Asian lands, namely that the former preferred to acquire men rather than women, and also adults rather than children, while with the latter the preferences tended to be reversed. It is known that the ratio of men to women exported by the Atlantic trade averaged about 2 to I, and something like the reverse of this ratio may be relevant to the Muslim trades. The consequence, bearing in mind that African societies were polygynous, was that the capacity for making good losses inflicted by an export slave trade would be higher where the trade was to the Americas than where it was to North Africa or Asia. Furthermore, of course, not all regions were equally touched by export slave trades, while some societies were more able than others to resist damage from a slave trade—or, indeed, to profit from it. In West Africa, for instance, there had been an essential continuity of population and population growth, and of social, economic and cultural evolution, ever since its inhabitants had embarked on agriculture and metallurgy some two or more millennia before the period of greatest slave-trading. Its societies, in Guinea as well as in the western Sudan, had commonly been accustomed to coping with—and trying to profit from—the demands of foreign traders before such traders came to demand slaves in any numbers. It may therefore be presumed that they were able to organize their affairs so as to minimize damage from slave trading. But to the east and south of the Cameroons, a new departure had been made with the coming of the Bantu-speakers who, for the most part, were the introducers of agriculture and metal-working. Except in so far as the northwestern Bantu had been able to maintain some cultural and economic continuity with nearby West Africa, and had also shared with it in the earliest expansion of European trade, and the people of a narrow band along the east coast and around the Zambezi valley had been touched by Indian Ocean trade, Bantu Africa had also been largely remote from outside trade or influence until it began to experience the dramatic increases in the Atlantic and Indian Ocean demands for slaves. It may be supposed, therefore, that it should have been more seriously affected by them. Yet there is some evidence, from Congo and Angola for example, to show that some affected populations did not decline in numbers, or that the combined effects of drought, famine and disease were as or more important than the export slave trade in restraining population growth.

For sub-Saharan Africa as a whole, perhaps only three generalizations are possible. First, that the export of people to other parts of the world, together with the concomitant indirect losses of life involved in slaving, was obviously a major constraint on population growth (though the further generalization that these things actually led to widespread depopulation needs closer

---

* See, for example, Colin Clark, *Population Growth and Land Use* (1967). After 1800, the demographers postulate an increasingly rapid growth of population, with a mean rate of annual increase of 0.19 per cent for the nineteenth century as a whole, until in the twentieth century one comes to the growth rates of around 3 per cent per annum that are now established for many African countries.

examination). Secondly, that it was essentially through the slave trade that sub-Saharan African societies were first brought into contact with the rapid changes that were occurring in the modern world as a consequence of the rise of western European economic power. Thirdly, that the combined effects of this enforced emigration of people and of this new contact with the outside world were a major force for change in Black Africa, and by the end of the eighteenth century and the beginning of the nineteenth, when export slaving reached its peak, probably the major force for change.

London: Emerging Global City of Empire (1660–1851)

by Dana Rabin

THE EMPIRE MANIFESTED IN LONDON

Our story begins with the end of the old City of London. From September 2 until September 5 in 1666 the Great Fire of London raged, destroying much of the city. Over 373 acres within the city itself and 63 acres beyond its walls were destroyed. At least one hundred thousand people lost their homes. Rebuilding the city coincided with a tremendous influx of people into the metropolis. The capital's population was nearly 630,000 in 1715, up from a half a million in 1674. By 1760 the city's population had grown to 740,000, and in 1815 it was estimated at 1.4 million. This number doubled by 1850. Of Europe's cities only Paris, France; Naples, Italy; and Istanbul, Turkey, came close to London in size. Despite these numbers, London's rate of growth was inconsistent: periods of demographic and economic stagnation alternated with booming expansion. Among the city's impoverished close quarters, poor hygiene and malnutrition contributed to high mortality rates. The city depended on constant in-migration for growth. Those who flocked to London looking for work were overwhelmingly young, and a full 25 percent of the nation's residents spent at least part of their lives (mostly in their youth, employed as servants) in the city's environs. Women outnumbered men. Immigrants were drawn to the city: Huguenots from France and other Protestants came to escape religious persecution; South Asian seamen, the lascars, were lured to London's port by the insatiable demand for skilled mariners; Irish men and women and young people from all over England and Scotland came to the city seeking employment; and enslaved persons were imported by their masters.

As befits the metropole of a global empire, the city's population was ethnically, religiously, economically, and racially diverse. Over the period covered in this chapter (1660–1851), the city was peopled largely by those from Scotland, Ireland, Wales, and England. During the last half of the eighteenth century, refugees came to Britain after the Seven Years' War, the American

Dana Rabin, "London: Emerging Global City of Empire (1660-1851)," *Places of Encounter: Time, Place, and Connectivity in World History, Volume Two: Since 1500,* ed. Aran MacKinnon and Elaine McClarnand MacKinnon, pp. 54-56. Copyright © 2012 by Taylor & Francis Group. Reprinted with permission.

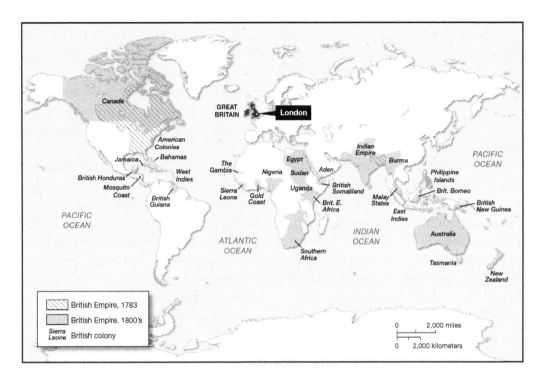

MAP 2.1. Growth of the British Empire

Britain emerged as a world empire through the international wars of the mid-eighteenth century. Although the American colonies gained their independence in 1783, Britain retained its lucrative colonies in the Caribbean, and over the next century its holdings grew to include Canada, South Asia, and parts of Africa, earning it the title "the Empire on which the sun never sets."

Revolutionary War, the French Revolution, and the Napoleonic Wars. In the 1830s and 1840s, migration brought political refugees exiled from repressive regimes. The well-known among them included Guiseppe Mazzini, Karl Marx, and the future Napoleon III. (Marx spent most of his time in the reading room of the British Library, where he wrote *Das Kapital*.) Many of London's immigrants settled first in the city's East End. Although this area was best known for the density of its Jewish population, Chinese and Irish immigrants settled there as well. As they became more established, the communities spread elsewhere in the metropolis. These constant new additions to the city's population imprinted London with cultural, intellectual, economic, and political influences.

The most obvious evidence of the entanglement of colonial and metropolitan Britain was the presence of some ten thousand to fifteen thousand people of African descent in the capital in the eighteenth century and estimates that up to five thousand blacks lived in other parts of England, most of them concentrated in Bristol and Liverpool. Britain's visual culture provides a rich record of black presence in eighteenth-century England, especially in the portraits of wealthy absentee landlords surrounded by their families, servants, and slaves. Masters brought enslaved Africans to London from Africa, the Caribbean, or the North American colonies, and free Africans who had emancipated themselves arrived at London's busy port after serving as sailors on slave ships or other British vessels. England's black population was overwhelmingly young, male, and transient. While many black men worked as sailors and soldiers, they also appear in visual sources as footmen, coachmen, pageboys, street vendors, and musicians, and they are mentioned in some criminal records as pimps, prostitutes, highway robbers, and beggars. The city was not segregated, and blacks and whites lived in close proximity, socialized together, and intermarried.

Another significant minority came from Britain's South Asian colonial territories. British trade in South Asia dated back to the early seventeenth century, and the contacts of colonialism in India, Cape Town, and Malacca brought many thousands of Indians to Britain as servants, scholars, students, royalty, officials, merchants, tourists, and settlers. Indian seamen, known as lascars, were the largest group. "Lascar" comes from the word *lashkar* or *khalasi*, the name for a crew or maritime labor gang hired by captains to work on their ships, so the term refers to their employment status rather than their ethnicity. Although the name as used by the English implied coherence among these immigrants from South and East Asia, the lascars were far from homogenous in terms of their ethnicity, religion, and caste backgrounds. Their labor built the expanding empire, especially in light of the shortage of experienced sailors, a consequence of the tremendous expansion of the British navy and no lack of opportunities for employment in global maritime trade.

The city's religious groups were also diverse. Some of the lascars were Muslims, and Romani (gypsies) and Irish Catholics who came to Britain to work as summer seasonal laborers found a winter home in London. The majority in the Protestant Church of England were joined by London's Catholic communities, which flourished especially toward the end of the eighteenth century. French Protestant Huguenots, who had been protected by the 1598 Edict of Nantes that granted them certain privileges, including religious liberty, fled to England with the edict's revocation in 1685. Two hundred thousand Huguenots left France for non-Catholic Europe. Fifty thousand Huguenots, many of them skilled craftsmen, sought refuge in England and ten thousand in Ireland. The modern term "refugee" has its origins in these events. Jews had been exiled from England by Edward II in 1250. Although they were never formally invited back or officially readmitted, Jews began to immigrate to England in the middle of the seventeenth century and comprised a growing population.

Questions for Reflection

In these Perspectives excerpts, the authors deal with intricate demographic issues to assess the impact of the slave trade on Africa. They also explore how London's growth mirrored trends in the British Empire. As you reflect on the significance of migrations and encounters, then and now, answer the following questions.

1. About when did the slave trade take off? What was the population of the continent of Africa at that time? South of the Sahara?

2. In demographic studies, what is "annual natural increase"? According to the authors, what is the correlation between this and the impact of slavery?

3. What, if any, were the differences between the European and Muslim slave trades? How do you account for those differences?

4. What three generalizations conclude this excerpt? What remaining questions come to mind?

5. What tragedy became a turning point in the growth and development of London?

6. Put together a short profile of London's growth and diversity. What two minority populations were linked to Britain's colonial empire?

7. How did London's growth change the character and identity of the city? Was the British Empire shaped by what was happening in London or the reverse? How does London's growth illustrate the importance seeing patterns of continuity and change over time?

8. Finally, what to you is the best way to understand the migrations and encounters featured in this chapter? What word would you use to describe what happened?

Activities Menu

Your instructor may assign one or more of the following learning activities:

Prewriting Exercise

Take a minute and write a paragraph (half page of notebook paper) on what you know about how the transatlantic slave trade impacted African societies.

Media

Select a relevant video program from one of the following and write a one-page (double-spaced) reaction.

- ＋ TED Talk
- ＋ Munk Debates
- ＋ C-SPAN
- ＋ Crash Course

Source Search

Select and read two related primary sources found at the Modern History Sourcebook and incorporate them into your essay.

Short Essay I

Write a three-page (double-spaced) essay of about 750 words in answer to the following question: Drawing on the material from this chapter, what were the most important migrations of the time (both voluntary and involuntary)? Why do you think that cities like London became the destination for such migrations? From what you can tell, how did contemporaries handle these encounters with unfamiliar peoples?

Short Essay II

Write a three-page (double-spaced) essay of about 750 words in answer to the following question: Compare the migrations of the early modern world noted in this chapter with immigration in the early 21st century in three ways: the reasons for migration, the ethnic composition of immigrants, and the impact on one or two destination cities or regions.

Role-Playing Exercise

The early modern world was built on the backs of African slaves. Select several students to assume the roles of contemporaries trying to confront the problem of the transatlantic slave trade. Would your argument be an economic one? Would it address political regimes that fostered the slave trade? Or would you argue for an end to the trade based on moral principle? Just as we try to stop human trafficking today against all odds, remember how difficult it was for contemporaries to address the entrenched financial and political interests of the time.

Quiz

Complete an objective quiz created by your instructor.

Suggested Reading

Alfred W. Crosby, *The Columbian Exchange: Biological and Cultural Consequences of 1492* (2003)

J.D. Fage and William Tordoff. "The First Stage of the Impact of World Trade on Tropical Africa," in *A History of Africa* (2002)

Stephen Gaukroger, *The Collapse of Mechanism and the Rise of Sensibility: Science and the Shaping of Modernity, 1680–1760* (2011)

Jonathan Israel, *Enlightenment Contested: Philosophy, Modernity, and the Emancipation of Man, 1670-1752* (2006)

Dana Rabin, "London: The Emerging Global City of Empire (1660–1851)," in *Places of Encounter: Time, Place, and Connectivity in World History, Volume Two: Since 1500* (2012)

Chapter 3

Chapter Skill	Making the Most of Comparisons
Chapter Issue	Cities & Revolution
Chapter Objectives (Students will...)	<ul><li>Identify three specific ways in which cities were integral to modern revolutions</li><li>Assess current perspectives on Paris and St. Petersburg as revolutionary cities</li><li>Demonstrate in a short essay on these two cities how we can make the most of historical comparisons</li></ul>
Assignments and Assessments	1. Read the Setup Narrative 2. Listen to the Lecture(s) 3. Read the Perspectives excerpts 4. Compose a three-page Essay in answer to the assigned prompt

Setup Narrative: Cities & Revolution

As we saw in the last chapter, understanding the modern West means understanding cities. This is especially true when we consider one of the major features of the modern world: revolution. A modern revolution without cities makes no sense.

Neither does one without ideas to inspire. After a century of religious wars ended in 1648, Europe was ready to turn its attention away from killing each other over salvation to rekindling societies based on science. Galileo Galilei embodies an age of worlds old and new: the new science in a tug-of-war with the claims of the Catholic Church. Galileo was eventually put under house arrest, but his ideas freely roamed about the labs and salons of Europe's elite, including its monarchs, who began competing over scientific patronage. It became a badge of honor to promote science, to be seen as an enlightened ruler. This was one of things that made the Scientific Revolution revolutionary. Another was that it gave us what may be the world's first *lingua franca*: the universal language of mathematics. Scientists and tinkerers from London to China's Liaodong Peninsula could now speak the same language about the cosmos and chemistry and their natural laws of the natural world. But then did such laws govern the human world, too? Had we missed them? Enlightenment figures of all sorts affirmed they could and should, and we had. John Locke on good government, Voltaire on religious toleration, Montesquieu on the separation of powers and their checks and balances, Adam Smith on free trade, Cesare Beccaria on criminology, and brave souls like Mary Wollstonecraft on women's rights—these came like rapid fire on the old regime in what's been called the Age of Reason, dispelling the darkness of ignorance. An age of light.

But it was also one of fire. Enlightenment ideas weren't mere décor, they challenged the legitimacy of absolute monarchs, the grip of religious discrimination, and the persistent lack of equality and social mobility, things that can shake a system to its core. And that's exactly what they did. Taken together, the Atlantic revolutions (the American, French, Haitian, and Spanish revolutions) and the two Russian revolutions of 1917 constitute an unmistakable turning point in the story of modern Western world. They represent a moment when subjects became citizens, citizens became popular representatives, and popular representatives themselves became rulers and builders of a new order. They took the ideas of popular sovereignty to the streets, the main streets and thoroughfares of Europe's capitals, to the heart of the respective regimes. That makes cities central to the stories of revolution, inseparable from them, and if we concentrate on Paris and St. Petersburg, which we will do in this chapter, we will see just how inseparable they are. You will work on a comparison of the French and Russian revolutions below, but to get you started, keep the following in mind: both were rebellions against monarchs who jealously guarded their right to rule and stubbornly resisted change; both rulers half-heartedly entertained reform measures; both were ousted from power by massive popular uprisings, ending lengthy dynasties; both were executed, and both were replaced by revolutionaries whose ideas upended their systems and challenged the rest of Europe to view the aims of the body politic in an entirely new light. Interestingly, despite revolution, both places ended up with authoritarian regimes. But there were significant differences, too. Geographically, France and Russia were and are night and day. The Bourbon dynasty was deeply beset by internal problems and France falteringly attempted to build a constitutional order. Russia fell in world war and then attempted to build a communist order. And though the French Revolution was a bloody affair, it pales in comparison to the Russian case.

That said, Paris and St. Petersburg (or, Petrograd at the time of the revolution) are nearly synonymous with the revolutions that seized them. Why is that? Answering that question is your task in this chapter.

Lecture
Pay attention to the chapter lecture(s), either online or in class.

Tips on Making the Most of Comparisons

 • Remember that there is nothing really new under the sun. The things that excite or rattle us did the same to generations of people before us, so let's learn from them!

26

- Know the times enough to be able to make useful comparisons. In this chapter, that means getting to know two cities so well you can clearly see things that are similar and others that are different.
- Make comparisons and draw conclusions about similar things: city to city, institution to institution, technology to technology. Comparing a medieval saint with a 21st century techie probably won't get you very far.

The City and the Revolution

by David Garrioch

PARISIAN SOCIETY AND REVOLUTION

Changes in social relations and government had made a revolution possible. Across the 1790s the character and dynamism of Parisian society continued to shape it. Only a city of some size could have provided the extraordinary human energy that the events of 1789 unleashed. For most of the decade Paris led and powered the Revolution. Many thousands of its citizens turned out to protest and to act in July 1789 and again in October. Up to 30,000 protested after the attempted flight of the royal family in July 1791. Close to 15,000 militants were active in the sections in late 1793 and rather more across the whole period of the Revolution. The members of committees gave up hundreds of hours of leisure and sleeping time to keep the city running and the wheels of revolution turning. Thousands served each week (not all of them willingly, it must be said) in the Garde nationale. The National Guard had over 116,000 members in early 1793—around two out of every three adult males in the city. The revolutionary armies recruited 7,000 volunteers who sometimes spent lengthy periods away from their jobs and families scouring the provinces for grain and for counterrevolutionaries. There were around 10,000 voters in the 1791 legislative elections; 14,000 for the election of the mayor in 1790, and slightly more in 1793. Given people's unfamiliarity with the process and the long and complex voting system, the fact that 15 to 20 percent of the electorate voted in any one election is not bad. (It could take several hours for the electoral officers to be chosen, the credentials of the voters checked, and the candidates voted on, one at a time.)[1]

But numbers were not the only factor. High levels of literacy and well-developed news networks were vital for political participation. So was the decay of the old patronage networks and the capital's relative openness to newcomers and to innovation. Neither the nobility nor the clergy ruled Paris. Nor, any longer, did the magistrates, officeholders, and wealthy merchants who had once been so powerful: even the once-dominant Parlement faded into obscurity overnight. The old power bases, founded on militia rank, local administration and patronage, guild government and family networks, had all crumbled.

The new political landscape was already visible in April 1789, when for the first time significant numbers of Parisians—those paying taxes to the value of 3 livres, about three days' wages for a laborer—got to elect their representatives. The men they chose were often new figures, with no power base in their quarters and no history of public office. The extent of the turnover is reflected in the small numbers of former churchwardens elected in 1789 and after: in the entire faubourg St-Antoine, which after 1790 was divided into three sections, only 6 former churchwardens were among nearly 200 men elected to section committees up to mid-1794.[2]

Some of the new men were schoolteachers, wine merchants, butchers; their occupations had been poorly represented among the old local elites. Even lawyers, who had made up less than 10 percent of the notables chosen to participate in elections at the Hôtel de Ville between 1775 and 1789, now formed over 40 percent of the Third Estate electors. An increasing number of the revolutionary leaders were migrants or sons of migrants whose energy and drive had enabled them to make successful careers in the big city: one was Antoine-Pierre Damoye, an entrepreneurial carriage maker who had diversified into carriage renting, haulage, and real estate.[3]

As the Revolution went on, the numbers of men drawn from outside the old political elite increased. Whereas during the Old Regime the officials of the trades and the parish church-wardens were almost all Paris-born or had been in the city for many years, in 1794 half of the members of the civil committee of the faubourg Montmartre section had been in Paris for less than eight years. And while seniority had been an important prerequisite for an Old Regime notable, now younger men began to play an active role, men like Nicolas-François Bellart, a twenty-two-year-old lawyer who was elected in April 1789 and subsequently became secretary of the Petit-St-Antoine district. He was exceptional, but across the city growing numbers of men in their thirties were elected to public office in the early 1790s.[4]

These newcomers were chosen on the basis less of rank, age, or family background (which was often unknown to many of the voters), but according to their reputation, words, and deeds. The idea that individual worth rather than birth should be the basis for public office was already widespread in the late Enlightenment and was now being put into action. It produced some unlikely leaders. Guillaume Bouland was one, a former servant who became a radical voice in the Observatoire section before winning office in the Finistère section, and who subsequently became a judge in the Paris courts. Just as unexpected was the appearance in a section commit-tee of Guillaume Carrel, a former dancer at the opera; or the career of the former postal clerk Jean Varlet, aged twenty-seven when he came to prominence in the radical Cordeliers Club.[5]

The Parisian Revolution was also precociously egalitarian. Very early, many of the districts displayed an extraordinary spirit of inclusion. "It is right for all citizens in turn to participate in the administration of the commune," felt the St-Marcel district committee, and that of St-Roch threatened to fine notables who did not attend meetings. In recruitment to the new citizen mili-tia—what was to become the National Guard— many districts welcomed volunteers of all ranks and at least two districts stressed the need for simple uniforms that all could afford.[6] These were attitudes rooted in the social and political environment of prerevolutionary Paris, where many artisans were well aware of events and felt they should have a say.

This fertile soil provided the seedbed for other ideas that took root in the course of the Revolution. Republicanism was inconceivable in 1789, and so was universal male suffrage. Yet the precocious appearance of such demands and the widespread support they attracted in Paris as early as 1791 are easier to comprehend if we recognize that the prerevolutionary city already provided a climate in which ordinary people felt themselves ready and able to be citizens. The same was true of the extraordinary outburst of patriotism that accompanied the initial outbreak of revolution in Paris, quickly developing into an unprecedented popular nationalism. The development of a national spirit has been very little studied, but responses to the Seven Years' War of 1756–63 and the appearance of the "patriot party" in the 1770s suggest that it had deep roots, particularly in Paris. The patriotism of these years was a secular mixture of Gallicanism and Jansenism. From the Jansenist belief that Church doctrine should be determined by the community of all true believers, not solely by the pope, the bishops, or the clergy, it was only a step to the conviction that the political sovereignty lay with the people, not with the king and his ministers.[7] Patriotism was inseparable from the growing sense that Parisians had of themselves as citizens of France, not simply subjects of the French king. The political experience of the refusals of sacraments, the Maupeou catastrophe, and distrust of the reforming efforts of the Paris police and other agencies led many people in the city to identify patriotism with hostility to despotism. In July 1789 despotism was symbolized by the king's dismissal of the ever-popular minister Necker and by the well-publicized machinations of the comte d'Artois, Madame de Polignac, and their supporters in what came to be called "the court party" or even "the aristocracy." "The nation asked for Necker to be retained," cried Camille Desmoulins in a famous speech in the Palais-Royal on 12 July 1789. "Could you be more insolently defied?" he asked, now identifying "the nation" with his Parisian audience. "After this coup they will stop at nothing, and they may perhaps be planning a Saint Bartholomew's massacre of patriots."[8]

But perhaps the clearest example of the influence of the urban environment on political events is the way many ordinary Parisian women responded to revolution. The march to Versailles on 5 October 1789 was largely the work of working women from the central market district and from the faubourg St-Antoine—areas linked by numerous work ties. Suspicious of the court and its supporters and firmly believing that the political opponents of the Third Estate were trying to prevent reform by driving up bread prices in Paris, these women gathered thousands of others around them and laid siege to the Hôtel de Ville. They expressed exasperation with the paper shufflers of the municipality, and one group tried to set fire to papers stored in the building, saying "that it was all that had been done since the Revolution began." They were equally scathing about their own menfolk: "these women repeated that the men were not strong enough to avenge themselves and that they would show themselves to be better than the men." "The men are holding back," said others, "the men are cowards . . . we will take over."[9] They did, marching 12 miles through the rain to the royal palace. They returned with promises of lower bread prices and of reform and brought the royal family with them as a guarantee.

This was the most dramatic women's action of the Revolution. But already, in September 1789, members of a deputation to the Hôtel de Ville seeking action on bread shortages and high prices were heard to say that "men did not understand anything about the matter and . .

. they wanted to play a role in affairs."[10] Later the market women were prominent in attacks on nuns whom they perceived to be counterrevolutionary, and in 1793 on radical women whose politics they equally condemned.

Other women were active in around a third of the popular societies and in many sectional assemblies, where they sometimes forced issues onto the agenda. In 1793 there were demands for female suffrage. Women of all ranks attended sittings of the National Assembly and maintained a noisy commentary on debates. The flexible and mobile nature of much female work enabled them to drop in as they were passing, and to listen while knitting or sewing. We know that women were among the most enthusiastic supporters of Robespierre and other key Jacobins, and of radicals like Jacques Hébert, Jacques Roux, Jean Varlet, and other lesser figures who fought to have ceilings placed on food prices. Women were active in most of the insurrectionary movements and finally revolted against the Jacobin leadership. Without their participation the Parisian Revolution would have been a very different affair. But without the independence that the social and economic environment of Paris gave women, and plebeian women in particular, it is hard to imagine them taking, from the very beginning and in large numbers, such independent action. Mary Wollstonecraft firmly believed, having visited Paris in 1794, that "from the enjoyment of more freedom than the women of other parts of the world, those of France have acquired more independence of spirit than any others."[11]

The nature of urban work and social relationships helped shape the distinctive political culture of revolutionary Paris. And revolutionary events helped activate the city's latent hostilities. Mistrust of merchants, and of bakers in particular, is well documented and erupted each time prices rose or shortages were experienced. It was exacerbated by breaches of communitarian ethics by the growing numbers of entrepreneurs for whom profit and consumer clienteles were more important than collective obligations to trade or neighborhood—and the turbulent 1790s provided ample opportunities for speculating of this sort. The Revolution gave older attitudes a new political dimension by making profiteering on necessities not only immoral but also unpatriotic. This outlook was not confined to Paris.

Popular anticlericalism too was not unique to Paris, but its vigor there was unusual. Here the continuities are not so clear, yet once again the character of the city was crucial. Clergy in Old Regime Paris, perhaps more than anywhere else, had to earn the respect of their congregation. A village priest might have a local monopoly, but in Paris dissatisfied parishioners could attend monastery churches, go to other parishes, and even not go to church at all. The Jansenist inheritance was again important. Going right back to the 1720s and 1730s, Parisians were accustomed to judging their clergy: there were "good" priests and "bad" ones (whether they belonged to the Jansenist opposition or to the "devout" anti-Jansenist party). Although there was no obvious continuity between Jansenist parishes and those where most of the clergy supported the Revolution, the distinction between "good" and "bad" priests reemerged in 1791, when roughly half the curés and just over a third of the ordinary parish clergy took the oath of loyalty to the constitution.[12]

Patriots found more bad apples among the religious orders, where only 42 percent took the oath. This confirmed an already widespread prejudice against the regular clergy, who were increasingly condemned in novels, philosophical literature, and popular story as corrupt, deca-dent, or at best a waste of potentially productive (and reproductive) citizens. Sentiments in Paris were mixed. Some of the religious orders worked closely with the local people: the Frères de la charité were well regarded by the printing workers for their care of the poor, and so were the Saint Vin-cent de Paul's Soeurs de la charité. Some, like the Franciscans, were strong supporters of the Revolution. At the same time, grocers and the fruit and butter merchants protested at unfair competition from religious houses. One Paris tanner was possibly putting a common view among the educated classes when he argued in his personal *cahier* in 1789 that monks should be made to do useful work teaching the city's children. A brewer suggested using the income of a number of abbeys to help the poor.[13]

These sentiments, openly expressed, may have strengthened the strand of anticlericalism that existed in prerevolutionary Paris. The very conservative stance of many of the clerical deputies to the Estates General did not help. In August 1789 a number of drunk people called out "A bas la calotte" (down with the priests) during a procession on the Ile-de-la-Cité, and there was outspoken public criticism of the archbishop's politics. In October, when thousands of Parisian women marched to Versailles, some of them invaded the benches of the National Assembly and shouted insults at the bishops, again to cries of "A bas la calotte!" Subsequently the pope's condemnation of the Revolution and the refusal of many clergy to take the oath of allegiance confirmed anticlericals in their prejudices.[14]

Just as significant in determining the fate of the Paris clergy, though, may have been indiffer-ence. Across the eighteenth century the role of the Church in Paris was declining. By the 1780s probably less than half the city's adult population took communion.[15] The Church's role in poor relief was diminishing as secular institutions intruded, and its capacity to provide assistance was lessening along with bequests, donations, and the contents of poor boxes and collection plates. The number of clergy was not keeping up with the growth in population and some Parisians had little contact with the Church.

In the climate of the 1790s, growing indifference or latent hostility to established religion allowed active anticlericalism to emerge and spread. Anticlericalism acquired legitimacy—even "patriotic" credentials—in declarations by public figures like Marat. Well before official perse-cution of "refractory" clergy began—late in 1791—there were attacks on nonjuror religious in Paris. In April groups of women broke into four convents and took whips to nuns hostile to the Revolution. The following year many priests were imprisoned as "suspects." The most horrific incidents took place in early September 1792 when a band of men went from prison to prison, apparently with the approval of members of the Commune, and battered to death between 1,100 and 1,400 people, including 220 clergy.[16] Most observers were horrified but afraid to intervene, and some public figures were prepared to excuse the violence. As political intimida-tion grew, the many who believed in freedom of religion were afraid to speak out. The active hostility many religious displayed toward the Revolution also made the defense of patriotic clergy increasingly difficult.

Nevertheless, dechristianization and anticlericalism were only ever minority movements in Paris. There were quite a number of priests like Jean-Jacques Poupart, the well-known curé of

St-Eustache, who remained in the city without being bothered.[17] Some of the two thousand nuns driven out of the convents adopted secular clothes but continued community life of a kind, and those who worked with the poor were sometimes defended by their sections.[18] As the political climate changed, in 1795, the churches were reopened, generally by lay people. The restorers of religion were not counterrevolutionaries though, since the churches they reestablished were mostly modeled on the revolutionary Constitutional Church of 1791. They often had a democratic structure, with priests elected by the parish council or in some cases by the entire congregation: as some Jansenists had suggested years before.

Revolutionary anticlericalism, therefore, was a product of the encounter between a long-lived strand of hostility to the Church, widespread indifference, and the particular crises of the 1790s. It illustrates once again the way that prerevolutionary social relations made possible and influenced the Parisian Revolution, yet without predetermining its course.

Sentiment against the nobility probably operated in a similar way. The pretensions of minor nobles were resented by much of the Paris "public," as the 1782 Moreton-Chabrillant incident demonstrated. A longstanding hostility in Paris to the court at Versailles grew acute in the late 1780s, holding the gilded courtesans and self-serving ministers responsible for the woes of Paris and providing a base for revolutionary antipathy to all nobles. There were already isolated threats against Parisian nobles in the middle of 1789. Once the court moved to Paris at the end of 1789, evidence of the numerous counterrevolutionaries within the king's entourage was right under the noses of Parisians. The king's bodyguard were the most unpopular and they clashed frequently with National Guardsmen on duty at the Tuileries palace. In February 1791 quite a number of noblemen at the Tuileries were disarmed by the National Guard following a rumor that they had been about to assassinate the king—further evidence of the population's distrust.[19]

As in the case of the clergy, growing feeling against nobles was probably assisted by widespread indifference. Of all the Parisian elites, nobles had least contact with the ordinary people. Only a handful played any role in the parish churches, and then mainly in an honorific capacity. With the possible exception of the duc d'Orléans, who seems to have attempted to build a power base in the city in 1789, there is little evidence that noble families had more than commercial contacts with the Paris middle classes. People had no reason to disbelieve reports of noble plots against the Revolution, and the fate of the haughty Parisian nobility was a matter of indifference to most of the population.

The Integration of The City and The Revolution

Across the late eighteenth century the integration of Paris and changes in the role of the local middle classes were undermining the quarter and the parish as political units and making them less inclusive social entities. The importance of the broader outlook that resulted became clear very early, when the districts quickly formed a central assembly of electors to coordinate their activity. The section representatives formed societies like the Club de l'Evêché and the Club de la Ste-Chapelle to coordinate their activity. Later the Jacobin and Cordeliers Clubs served the same function. Especially after the beginning of 1790, frequent deputations went from district to district and subsequently between the sections. The local leaders were well aware of the way their counterparts elsewhere in the city were thinking and were very conscious of the need to act in unison.[20]

Crowd action too repeatedly transcended local interests and boundaries, displaying a new, citywide approach to politics. Already in April 1789 the Réveillon affair, with its appeals by the population of the faubourg St-Antoine to workers elsewhere in the city, had shown the potential for united action. In mid-July 1789 the same interplay of local and citywide action occurred. The Hôtel de Ville, where the Assembly of Electors was meeting, was the focal point to which the crowds from all over the city returned repeatedly on 12, 13, and 14 July. The takers of the Bastille were primarily people from the faubourg St-Antoine and the neighborhoods immediately adjoining the fortress but included a significant number from other parts of the city, once again particularly from the faubourg St-Marcel. Again on 20 June 1792 citizens from all over the city gathered—with little central organization—to force the king to reinstate the popular ministers he had just dismissed.[21]

These acts had no direct prerevolutionary precedents but were prepared by the city's growing integration and the sense of interdependence that it created. By the 1780s changing uses of urban space were breaking down the psychological and social boundaries between quarters and preparing the way for the citizens' coordinated action.

At the same time, the remarkable local commitment displayed by many of these same people suggests the incompleteness of the city's integration. In July 1789 the defense of the city against possible military attack was conducted on a local basis. While the notables of the district committees organized citizen militia units groups of neighbors spontaneously prepared to repel the expected assault. "The women and children took up the paving stones in the courtyards to attack these traitors to the *patrie* from the windows," wrote a café owner near St-André-des-Arts.[22]

In the following weeks and months lawyers, priests, and merchants, many of them active participants in the new metropolitan culture, reassumed responsibility for food supply, law and order, streetlighting and maintenance, public health, and later poor relief. The boundaries of districts and subsequently of sections took on an administrative and political significance that local divisions of the city had not had for over a century. And even after the initial emergency was over, the local leaders fought to retain their role, onerous as it was. One of the characteristics of both the districts and the sections was their jealous defense of local sovereignty, which repeatedly brought them into conflict with the municipality, the National Assembly, and with one another.[23]

At times they almost literally drew the wagons into a circle around their own enclave. On 25 June 1792, at a time of high tension following renewed rumors of a planned coup by the court, the St-Marcel battalion of the National Guard was summoned by the tocsin to its parade ground in the old cloister. Scouts were sent out into the streets leading toward the city center and returned with news that the area was surrounded by troops loyal to the court. The battalion spent the entire day under arms, its cannon loaded and covering the cloister's entrances.[24] There was in fact no such plot and no army units preparing to attack. Even if there had been, they would hardly have been likely to pay much attention to the outlying faubourg St-Marcel. But the incident illustrates a strong sense that the areas beyond the narrow boundaries of their quarter were potentially hostile.

The popular movement also kept the customary mentality characteristic of the neighborhood communities of the city, often placing collective rights above individual ones within a local context. It remained bitterly opposed to the principles of economic liberalization that dominated successive National Assemblies. The "grocery riots" of 1792, when crowds seized sugar and coffee from warehouses in many parts of the city and sold it at a "just" price, are often passed over as "traditional" forms of protest somehow inconsistent with the "modern" revolutionary political culture. But they were perfectly at one with the aims of social justice that were central to the popular movement. The short-lived victory of that movement in 1793 marked the temporary triumph of this same mentality, particularly with the introduction of a ceiling on the prices of a surprisingly wide range of "necessities." This "maximum" was a measure that militants had sought repeatedly, using all the new techniques of revolutionary action.

Thus the Parisian Revolution was shaped in numerous ways by the long-term evolution of the city. Yet while continuities of all sorts were present, I am not suggesting that its course was predetermined, or wishing to downplay the remarkable changes it wrought. The springs of revolutionary thought and action lay in the past, but the Revolution operated an extraordinary transformation, opening up possibilities previously glimpsed only in dreams. There was little in the prior lives of individual Parisians to indicate what choices each would make when faced with a more dramatic upheaval than most human beings ever have to confront.

Some forms of revolutionary action went far beyond anything the eighteenth-century history of the city would lead us to expect. In October 1789 the women's march to Versailles, though rooted in the community of the central markets, gathered women from all over the city and far exceeded in size, aims, and consequences anything that had happened in the eighteenth century. The republican petition of the Champ de Mars, which five thousand people signed in 1791 to demand the dismissal of the king, was likewise startlingly new, transcended local boundaries, and foreshadowed the techniques of nineteenth- and twentieth-century political movements. On 10 August 1792 the military attack on the royal palace that overthrew the monarchy was an example of coordination and united political purpose worthy of twentieth-century revolutions. In these revolutionary actions we can detect elements of a new political consciousness, of an emerging sense of class, in some instances of modern feminism and of nineteenth-century popular nationalism. These were above all products of the revolutionary context, scarcely detectable within the prerevolutionary population.

Late-eighteenth-century Paris was moving out of a world structured by deference and hierarchy into one governed overwhelmingly by money and appearances. The collective sanctions, limited horizons, and customary culture of small communities were being complemented and modified by wider sources of identity and legitimacy—class and nation. Personal monarchy was giving way to an abstract state. Collective rights were being superseded by individual rights. In all of these areas Parisian society was precocious, because of its dynamic market economy, its relatively large population, and its function as capital. It was only in such a place, already a locus of social, economic, and political experimentation, a city unlike any other in Europe, that revolution could have taken place in the form it did. And the Revolution took this extraordinary city and transformed it still further.

Notes

1. Reinhard, *Nouvelle histoire de Paris,* 230, 258–59, 318–19.
2. Robert Barrie Rose, "How to Make a Revolution: The Paris Districts in 1789," *Bulletin of the John Rylands University Library* 59 (1977): 441, 448049; LL836, vestry of Ste-Marguerite, 1759–88; Raymonde Monnier and Albert Soboul, *Répertoire du personnel sectionnaire parisien en l'an II* (Paris, 1985), 271–82, 283–94, 295–310.
3. Maurice Genty, *Paris 1789–1795: l'apprentissage de la citoyenneté* (Paris, 1987), 21; K996–97, elections of municipality, 1776–89; Richard Mowery Andrews, "Paris of the Great Revolution, 1789-1796," in *People and Communities in the Western World,* ed. Gene Brucker (Homewood, Ill., 1979), 73.
4. Richard Mowery Andrews, "Social Structures, Political Elites and Ideology in Revolutionary Paris, 1792-1794: A critical evaluation of Albert Soboul's *Sans-culottes parisiens en l'an II," Journal of Social History* 19 (1985-86): 86; Rose, "How to Make a Revolution," 448–49; Garrioch, *Parisian Bourgeoisie,* 163–64.
5. Georges Garrigues, *Les districts parisiens pendant la Révolution française* (Paris, 1931), 22, 169–71; Garrioch, *Parisian Bourgeoisie,* 157–81; Robert Barrie Rose, *The Enragés: Socialists of the French Revolution* (University Park, Pa., 1968), 10–35.
6. BN Lb40 1621, district de St-Marcel: *Assemblée générale de la Commune dudit District, pour le mardi 1er septembre 1789* (n.p., [1789]); Garrigues, *Districts parisiens,* 22, 169–71.
7. Dziembowski, *Nouveau patriotisme français;* Van Kley, *Religious Origins,* 255–60; McManners, *Church and Society,* 2:672–78.
8. Antoine-Joseph Gorsas, *Le courrier de Versailles à Paris et de Paris à Versailles,* 13 July 1789; Edward Rigby, *Letters from France,* ed. Elizabeth Rigby Eastlake (London, 1880), 12 July 1789; Desmoulins's speech quoted in Jacques Godechot, *The Taking of the Bastille, 14th July 1789,* trans. Jean Stewart (New York, 1970), 187–88.
9. *Procédure criminelle,* witness 81; Olwen Hufton, *Women and the Limits of Citizenship in the French Revolution* (Toronto, 1992), 16; and idem, *The Prospect Before Her,* 473; Darlene Gay Levy and Harriet B. Applewhite, "Women of the Popular Classes in Revolutionary Paris, 1789-1795," in *Women, War and Revolution,* ed. Carol R. Berkin and Clara M. Lovett (New York, 1980), 15.
10. Hardy, "Mes loisirs," BN ms fr. 6687, fol. 469.
11. Godineau, *Citoyennes tricoteuses,* esp. 116–53; Dominique Godineau, "Le rapport masculin-féminin dans l'espace urbain (Paris XVIIIe siècle-Révolution française)" in *Marseillaises: les femmes et la ville,* ed. Yvonne Knibiehler et al. (Paris, 1993), 112–14; Mary Wollstonecraft, *An Historical and Moral View of the Origins and Progress of the French Revolution and the Effect It Has Produced in Europe,* 2d ed. (London ,1795), 425–26.
12. Reinhard, *Nouvelle histoire de Paris,* 196–97.
13. Ibid., 189–91,197; John McManners, *The French Revolution and the Church* (London, 1969), 8-10; Contat, *Anecdotes typographiques,* 78; Chassin, *Elections et les cahiers,* 2:482, 522, 545; Ba 64A, dossier 2, fols. 1–5.
14. BN ms fr. 6687, fols. 435, 436.
15. McManners, *French Revolution and the Church,* 11.
16. Célestin Guittard de Floriban, *Journal de Célestin Guittard de Floriban, bourgeois de Paris sous la Révolution* , ed. Raymond Aubert (Paris, 1974), 41; McManners, *French Revolution and the Church,* 62.
17. Ménétra, *Journal of My Life,* 224 n. 287.
18. Jean Boussoulade, "Les religieuses et les serments," *Annales historiques de la Révolution française* 25 (1953): 127, 133; and idem, "Soeurs de charité et commissaires de bienfaisances des

faubourgs Saint-Marcel et Saint-Antoine (septembre 1793–mai 1794)," *Annales historiques de la Révolution française* 200 (1970): 350–74.

19. Reinhard, *Nouvelle histoire de Paris,* 167–68; Guittard de Floriban, *Journal,* 28; Patrice Higonnet, *Class, Ideology and the Rights of Nobles during the French Revolution* (Oxford, 1981), 83–84.

20. *Compte rendu des séances électorales de 1791 et de la division du Corps électoral en deux sociétés, sous les noms de Club de l'Evêché, Club de la Ste-Chapelle* (Paris, 1791); Garrigues, *Districts,* 51.

21. Rudé, *The Crowd in the French Revolution,* 58–59, 100–101.

22. Letter of Joseph Carol, 18 July 1789, in G. Capon, ed., "La prise de la Bastille: lettre inédite," *Intermédiaire des chercheurs et des curieux* 86 (1923): cols. 517–20.

23. Richard Cobb, *The Police and the People* (Oxford, 1970), 122.

24. Jacques Godechot, "Fragments des mémoires de Charles-Alexis Alexandre sur les journées révolutionnaires de 1791 et 1792," *Annales historiques de la Révolution française* 24 (1952): 182.

St. Petersburg: The Russian Revolution and the Making of the Twentieth Century (1890–1918)

by Elaine McClarnard MacKinnon

PRELUDE TO REVOLUTION: INDUSTRIALIZATION, MODERNIZATION, AND WORLD WAR

St. Petersburg in 1917 was the largest city in the Russian Empire, with an estimated 2.4 million inhabitants. In addition to being the political and administrative capital, it was a major center for banking, commerce, and manufacturing. As a port city connected to the Baltic Sea, St. Petersburg served as the trade entrepôt for the whole empire, linking Russia to the world through its railway terminals and grain and stock exchanges. St. Petersburg was a religious capital as well, with major Orthodox Christian cathedrals, but, as a reflection of Russia's multinational makeup, it also became a focal point for Islam in the early twentieth century with the building of the Cathedral Mosque, the largest in Europe.

Also starkly visible were the inequities that fueled Russia's revolutionary upheaval. Its neighborhoods embodied the extremes of imperial grandeur and mass impoverishment characterizing tsarist society. Aristocratic families enjoyed palatial homes and apartments in the central districts, while just across the Neva, within view, were the crowded, unhealthy, working-class slums of the Vyborg district, ridden with mud, raw sewage, and poor roads. What distinguished St. Petersburg was the fact that the rich and the poor lived in close proximity to each other, heightening awareness of the gulf between them. Unlike in major cities such as London, Paris, and Berlin, neighborhoods segregated by class did not develop to the same extent in St. Petersburg, partly due to the inadequate development of public transportation. The poor had to be able to walk to work, and since most of the factories built after 1860 were located in or near the central city and its islands, this meant that the majority of the population lived within the official city limits. Thus, they saw on a daily basis the luxurious dwellings and the impressive imperial palaces owned by the aristocracy and upper-middle-class residents, who, unlike their counterparts in the West, did not move out to suburban areas. Class segregation did exist, but was not as much by neighborhoods as by floors. Even in the wealthiest districts one could find rich and poor sharing the same building. But the poor found themselves living in the wretchedly damp and cold cellars, which were frequently flooded, or on the very top floors, which had perpetually leaking ceilings. Also located within such prestigious neighborhoods as the Admiralty were large military garrisons. Segregation existed there in terms of public access—garrison soldiers and worker-migrants from the countryside found themselves barred, along with dogs, from parks and gardens.

What exacerbated these extremes was the explosive industrial growth that began after the emancipation of the serfs in 1861. By 1913 St. Petersburg housed nearly one thousand factories for industries that included metalworking, paper and printing, and food production. There was hardly any section of the city where you could not at least see or smell a factory or mill. This fueled in turn a major increase in population. Between 1850 and 1914 the city's population expanded from a little over five hundred thousand to more than two million. The increase was mainly due to the seasonal influx of thousands of migrants from the countryside who came seeking work; slightly less than one-third of the city's inhabitants in 1910 had been born in St. Petersburg. Many of these laborers were unmarried, male, and unfamiliar with the urban environment. Rural migration into the city and the workforce was certainly not an unusual pattern in global industrialization. But what distinguished the Russian case and contributed to volatility was the fact that the rural migrants retained close ties to their home villages, often returning seasonally to work in the fields and retaining proprietary rights in the village. This meant that urban workers remained in close touch with the problems and resentments of the countryside, where peasants fumed over high taxes and inadequate allotments of land. It also slowed the process of assimilation into urban mores and habits.

An additional source of tension was the fact that the urban population was growing exponentially but municipal services lagged considerably. St. Petersburg stood far behind comparable cities such as Berlin, New York, and Paris in the development of adequate housing, clean water, or transportation. Thousands were homeless, and in 1914 as many as one-fourth of inhabitants did not have access to running water. The central quarters of the city were so congested that some had to rent a hallway, or even a single corner or a bed in a room. The number of people living within single apartments was twice what it was in Paris or Vienna. The naturally cold and damp climate exacerbated the misery of the poor. The urban environment with its filthy cesspools and polluted water triggered perpetual outbreaks of cholera, typhus, diphtheria, tuberculosis, and pneumonia. Consequently, death rates in St. Petersburg exceeded those of any other major city in the Russian Empire, Europe, or the United States.

But the revolution was not just about poverty. St. Petersburg was at the forefront of Russian urbanization (less than one-fifth of the empire's population lived in cities in 1914) and in rising labor militancy. Nearly 70 percent of its population could read and write in 1910, which was double the rate found in most parts of Russia, though still well below the 90 percent rate found in Britain, France, Norway, and Sweden. Through growing access to modern forms of mass media—particularly the press—literate workers increasingly knew about gains being made by their counterparts in England and Western Europe, such as the right to strike, an eight-hour workday, and collective bargaining. It is also significant that St. Petersburg had the highest concentrations of workers in the world; factories tended to be much larger than they were in the United States and Europe and employed more persons. More than two-thirds of the city's workforce labored in enterprises with more than a thousand workers, including the Putilov Metal Works that employed over thirteen thousand. Workers' close proximity at home and work facilitated the spread of radical ideas, such as those circulating from European socialist parties and trade union movements that encouraged a greater sense of class consciousness and the entitlement of workers to rights, respect, and greater control over the conditions of their labor. Russian Menshevik and Bolshevik agitators consciously targeted these large enterprises with high concentrations of both skilled and unskilled laborers and found them to be prime recruiting grounds for teaching Marxist notions of class struggle and egalitarianism. Workers in these enterprises developed a strong class identity and embraced symbols of European socialism, such as May Day celebrations honoring labor. Among the most militant sectors in 1917 were the highly concentrated northern industrial areas across the Neva from the Winter Palace—the Vasilevsky, Petersburg and Vyborg districts.

The city had already been a cauldron for revolution in 1905, when desires for social justice and political liberalization drove workers, peasants, and middle-class elites to try unsuccessfully to overthrow Tsar Nicholas II. The tsarist regime survived thanks to the continued loyalty of the military and minor liberal concessions, including establishment of Russia's first parliament, the State Duma. But, weak in mind and will, Nicholas II could not accept his role as a constitutional monarch and refused to work with the Duma. He wanted Russia to stay politically and socially what it had been for centuries, a society dominated by the aristocracy, but due to modernization there were factory workers and middle-class professionals demanding rights and representation in public affairs. His oppressive responses to strikes and mass discontent earned him the nickname "Nicholas the Bloody."

What brought Russia to the brink of revolution again in 1917 was a confluence of these conditions of political discontent and social inequity with the outbreak of war in 1914. World War I for Russia was a disaster that brought catastrophic losses, inflation, and bureaucratic bungling. Early enthusiasm for the war quickly dissipated as the casualties mounted (over four million by August 1915), as did food and fuel shortages. The war disrupted railway service—the lifelines of the city that delivered its food, coal, iron, and oil. Nicholas II compounded the situation by taking over command of the armies and leaving political control largely in the hands of his wife, Empress Alexandra, and her disreputable adviser, the Siberian "holy man" Grigory Rasputin. This peasant-born healer had won Alexandria's undying devotion through his uncanny ability to

38

control the bleeding of her only son and Nicholas's heir, Alexei, who suffered from hemophilia. But Rasputin's dissolute behavior and political incompetence discredited the regime even further. Nicholas rejected efforts of the Duma and other public organizations to assist in the war effort. Major defeats in battle led to serious losses of territory and of men. By 1916 over five million soldiers were either dead, wounded, or had been taken prisoner. The tsar's disastrous leadership alienated every sector of society, including the highest ranks of the Russian military.

Web Resources

Alexander Palace Guide to Russian History Websites, www.alexanderpalace.org/index.html.

Alexander Palace Time Machine, www.alexanderpalace.org/palace/.

The Empire That Was Russia: The Prokudin-Gorskii Photographic Record Recreated, www.loc.gov/exhibits/empire/.

Mapping Petersburg, http://stpetersburg.berkeley.edu/index.html.

Nevsky Prospect photographs from pre–World War I, http://stpetersburg.berkeley.edu/olga/olga_splash.html.

The Russian Revolution: A Gallery of Photos, www.nevsky88.com/SaintPetersburg/Revolution/.

Saint Petersburg 1900: A Travelogue, www.alexanderpalace.org/petersburg1900/intro.html, including a photograph of the Nevsky Prospect, www.alexanderpalace.org/petersburg1900/36.html.

Seventeen Moments in Soviet History, www.soviethistory.org/.

Virtual Tour of St. Petersburg, www.saint-petersburg.com/virtual-tour/index.asp.

Questions for Reflection

In these two excerpts, the authors present a host of ways Paris and St. Petersburg illustrate the close relationship between cities and revolution. As you reflect on them, and compare urban revolutions generally, then and now, answer the following questions.

1. What are some ways that older Parisian identities (the quarter and parish, for example) were being overcome by new means of urban integration?

2. Note a couple of crowd actions that illustrate coordinated revolutionary efforts. Find a good contemporary map of Paris and locate the sites mentioned in the excerpt.

3. According to the authors, Parisian social and political integration was effective but it wasn't complete. What are some examples of this? How did moments like this affect the course of the revolution, if at all?

4. Describe the features of St. Petersburg (renamed Petrograd during World War I) as the capital of the Russian Empire.

5. What are good examples of the city's inequalities? How did Russian industrialization and urbanization compound these problems?

6. What was the impact of WWI?

7. As you compare these excerpts, what similarities do you see between Paris and Petrograd? What were their differences? How does this historical comparison deepen our understanding of both revolutions?

8. After answering the questions above, what to you is still unclear about these cities and their revolutions?

Activities Menu

Your instructor may assign one or more of the following learning activities:

Prewriting Exercise

Select either the French or Russian revolution and write a paragraph (half page of notebook paper) on what you know about the major problems that created conditions for a popular uprising.

Media

Select a relevant video program from one of the following and write a one-page (double-spaced) reaction.

- TED Talk
- Munk Debates
- C-SPAN
- Crash Course

Source Search

Select and read two related primary sources found at the Modern History Sourcebook and incorporate them into your essay.

Short Essay I

Write a three-page (double-spaced) essay of about 750 words in answer to the following question: Drawing on the material from this chapter, compare Paris and St. Petersburg as revolutionary cities. In what specific ways did they represent the tensions of the time in France and Russia? How did events and trends in these cities set the tone for wider revolution?

Short Essay II

Write a three-page (double-spaced) essay of about 750 words in answer to the following thesis. Defend or refute: "Paris and St. Petersburg are still revolutionary cities. The things that sparked revolution in Paris in 1789 and in St. Petersburg (or Petrograd) in 1917 cause occasional clashes today as well." In your answer, point to specific issues and trends.

Role-Playing Exercise

Select Paris or St. Petersburg and divide the class into revolutionary factions (using the Modern History Sourcebook or similar online document collection for background and additional content).

Have a couple of students represent each faction's agenda based on the conditions in the selected city. For whom do they speak? How (by what means) would they go about realizing their ideals?

Suggested Reading

Suzanne Desan, Lynn Hunt, and William Max Nelson, *The French Revolution in Global Perspective* (2013)

Philip Dwyer and Peter McPhee, eds., *The French Revolution and Napoleon: A Sourcebook* (2002)

Orlando Figes, *A People's Tragedy: The Russian Revolution, 1891–1924* (1996)

David Garrioch, "The City and the Revolution," in *The Making of Revolutionary Paris* (2002)

Elaine McClarnard MacKinnon, "St. Petersburg: The Russian Revolution and the Making of the Twentieth Century (1890–1918)," in *Places of Encounter: Time, Place, and Connectivity in World History, Volume II: Since 1500* (2012)

Chapter 4

Chapter Skill	Reasoning Chronologically
Chapter Issue	Industry & Poverty
Chapter Objectives (Students will...)	<ul><li>Identify three specific ways in which industrialization and poverty have historically been related</li><li>Assess one current perspective of the complicated relationship between industry and poverty</li><li>Demonstrate in a discussion on industry and poverty the ability to reason chronologically</li></ul>
Assignments and Assessments	1. Read the Setup Narrative 2. Listen to the Lecture(s) 3. Read the Perspectives excerpt 4. Take part in a role-playing Class Discussion 5. Take the Midterm Exam

Setup Narrative: Industry & Poverty

No development affected more people more fundamentally in modern history than the Industrial Revolution. Compared to other contemporary upheavals, it was unique. The American Revolution gave birth to constitutional government, and, while the French Revolution inspired nation-states, the Industrial Revolution transformed nearly everything, from grandiose visions of a better society down to the common, everyday rhythms of daily existence.

The Industrial Revolution was fastened together by new machines and technology. Each innovation advanced this fundamental economic transition from manual to mechanical power in its own way. The textile industry was first. By the mid-1780s, Hargreaves' jenny spun yarn and Cartwright's loom powered cloth detailing, reaching impressive new levels of production about the same time the iron workers found ways to fashion wrought iron out of the ore so abundant in England and northern swaths of Europe. Before the end of that same decade, Boulton and Watt built a steam engine that put the Industrial Revolution on track to remake industry and now transportation. Within two decades, a transportation revolution began as Trevithick's engine began to huff and puff around the Welsh countryside. Stephenson's improvement opened up a line from Liverpool to Manchester and serves as a major 1830 milestone, even if his *Rocket* could only manage five miles per hour. By 1850, major European states had hundreds of miles of track down, and the railroad industry became the symbol of an advanced, industrial society. This new age in the modern West ran on the rails of industry.

The Industrial Revolution turned out new kinds of societies as well as loads of manufactured goods. Inventors, entrepreneurs, and workers made the Industrial Revolution. They all played a part, but they rarely sang in unison. Inventors took the science of past decades and concerned themselves with applied technology. The entrepreneurs, often middling merchants from dissenting religious communities (denied careers in the professions and government for that reason), secured the necessary capital, purchased machines, ran the factories and mines, and employed workers. The new economic and social networks were horizontal rather than vertical, as they had been for most of the Middle Ages. Hence we begin to see the emergence of a middling rank, or middle class, equipped with political as well as economic ambitions. All of this depended on those who actually did the work, laborers with backgrounds as different as the points of the map they hailed from. Many came from nearby farms and countryside villages, and their arrival at factory towns and cities was, for them, a revelation in addition to a revolution. As competition increased, so did pressure to hold down the one thing factory managers could control: wages. As much as anything else, this revealed the vulnerability of those whose new routines consisted of long hours, monotony, tyrannical supervision, and neglected working conditions for low pay, or irregular pay, or no pay if infractions recorded in working books were serious enough. No population was more vulnerable in this new economic world than children, and the novels of Charles Dickens paint a vivid picture of this bleak house existence if ever one was needed. Apparently it was.

Toward the end of the 19th century, a New York police reporter named Jacob Riis published an exposé on industrial life that showed how the other half lived. For those with eyes to see, it presented a side of the city—and the Western world—that many would rather have avoided. Subsequent responses to the upheaval of industrialization fell into three types. Retool—embrace the new economic means with a hands-off, or *laissez faire*, approach. Reform—push for legislation and social reform to cut away the worst abuses of this new productive order. And then revolution, which saw reform as futile, if not worse. All three came in shades, but especially the latter. A new set of "-isms" emerged, the most radical being socialism and then a peculiar type of socialism, Marxism. How can industrial technology serve the entire community? This was the question socialism tried to answer. In time, what began as a response to the ideals and ills of industrialization turned into a long-term systemic competition between capitalism and communism that reached far into the 20th century.

Industrial society also reached far beyond the borders of Europe and made its revolution a global phenomenon. India and Egypt were drawn into the British economic orbit and saw their older economies turned into hubs for raw materials. Both came to stand for traditional societies that were faced with a major challenge: should they try to fend off dynamic imperial powers or should they adapt to Western ways and risk losing native identities? If that wasn't enough, it seemed that this unprecedentedly productive economy exported from Europe was importing poverty in new ways and on a new scale. Was that the case? Consider that as you read the excerpt below.

Lecture
Pay attention to the chapter lecture(s), either online or in class.

Tips on Reasoning Chronologically

+ This is a case where dates matter! To be able to put things in sequence, we must know when they happened.
+ This is also a case where logic matters. Normally there is some logic to a sequence of events. In this chapter, that means that the application of steam power during industrialization had to follow the discovery of related scientific principles. You engineers know this better than I do.
+ Try to understand one historical development after another. Don't jump ahead too much or you'll miss too much.

Industrialization, Imperialism, and World Poverty, 1750–1945

by Steven M. Beaudoin

POVERTY IN THE DEPENDENT ECONOMIES

Imperialism ensured that the parts of the world that did not undergo industrialization were nonetheless thrown into turmoil by this significant transformation, for it is impossible to understand the former outside the context of the latter. Industrialization increased the demand for raw materials in places like Western Europe, Japan, and the United States, while providing them the technology for securing those resources regardless of indigenous desires. With their newfound power, they imposed an international division of labor that made the non-industrialized world the producers of less expensive raw materials and the consumers of foreign manufactured goods. To achieve this new imbalance, which left the rest of the world either directly or indirectly dependent upon industrialized nations and the vagaries of the world economy, imperialist powers destroyed traditional economic systems during the final decades of the nineteenth century and then set about creating new structures that better served their interests. Drawing the connection between industrialization and imperialism even tighter, some scholars have adopted a Marxist model for analyzing this development and portray the producers of primary export products as the world's proletariat. While there was no one path to that outcome, the result increased both poverty and vulnerability around the globe.

The process of devastating more or less independent economies typically began by impoverishing the states that protected the autonomy of their markets and systems of production. In some areas, like India and sub-Saharan Africa, Europeans achieved this via outright domination and displacement of traditional rulers. In regions where indigenous sovereigns retained at least nominal independence, like China and the Ottoman empire, industrialized nations used a combination of military might and indebtedness to achieve their goals. Usually, this entailed massive foreign loans for embattled sultans, pashas, and emperors who sought to retain control by embarking on their own expensive modernization projects. Unfortunately, when it became impossible to make payments, the industrial powers stepped in to enforce payment, often by demanding oversight of internal finances. This occurred, for example, in both Egypt and the Ottoman empire during the 1870s, and ended with British control of the Nile and the creation of the Ottoman Public Debt Administration in 1881, a European-dominated institution that oversaw Ottoman assets as a guarantee on debt. At times, when foreign interference sparked open opposition to imperial encroachment, indemnities added to the crushing weight of debt. In China, foreign loans and compensation payments for the Opium Wars and Boxer Rebellion simply overwhelmed the Qing dynasty. The inability to control their own tariff income, the product of the unequal treaties signed in the mid-nineteenth century, hindered the government even further, as did the creation of concession areas where Chinese leaders were powerless to tax the fortunes being made from foreign trade and development. In each of these regions, internal political decline or colonial rule had similar impacts: traditional safety nets for those in need, which typically rested on elite support, became less secure; entitlements underwent drastic alterations; and states proved ineffective in preventing the mass poverty that followed in the wake of imperialism.

Industrialized nations employed two principal strategies for reducing the viability of independent economies once encroachment began. The first, the alienation of native rights to natural resources, typically followed the assertion of colonial control. Often this was accomplished by forcibly removing indigenous populations. In Southern Rhodesia, for example, Europeans expropriated over 15 percent of the land, more than 16 million acres, within the first decade of colonization. In South Africa, in 1913, whites restricted African ownership of land to special reserves comprising only 13 percent of the territory. Since available land in these areas could not meet population growth, widespread poverty developed. Many had no choice but to move to urban slums in search of jobs or to contract themselves out to white farmers as either laborers or sharecroppers. Still others found punishing employment in the vast diamond and gold mines established in southern Africa. In other parts of sub-Saharan Africa, Europeans forced subsistence farmers off of the land by levying taxes. Since colonial officials assessed these by head and not on income, smallholders were hit hardest. Once they fell into debt, they had little choice but to sell their land. In many parts of East Africa, large plantations arose to take the place of smaller farms, while in other areas, commercial agriculture based on sharecropping became the norm. Latin America witnessed a similar dynamic, which displaced autonomous indigenous communities in places like Mexico and Argentina, where small-scale local commerce had previously coexisted with large commercial farms dependent on world markets. Of course, in Latin America, plantations were nothing new. Building on a solid foundation established between 1500 and 1750, creole elites expanded their control over vast stretches of land thanks to an influx of European and American capital after 1870. For a growing segment of the populations of both Latin America and sub-Saharan Africa, then, it became increasingly difficult to make a living outside of the world economy. Moreover, as we will see in greater detail below, new economic structures only enhanced people's susceptibility to poverty.

In civilizations with more integrated commercial economies and a fully developed manufacturing sector (in the forms of both urban crafts and cottage industry), imperialism triggered impoverishment by altering customary trading patterns and fostering deindustrialization, the second strategy for decimating traditional economic systems. West Africa once prospered from trans-Saharan trade, for example, but colonizers brought this to an end and reoriented markets toward the Atlantic. As for manufacturing, in 1750, India and China produced 24.5 percent and 32.8 percent of the world's manufactured goods respectively; by 1860 those figures had fallen to 8.6 percent and 19.7 percent and in 1913 they were 1.4 percent and 3.6 percent. During the same span of time, the industrial nations' share rose from 27 percent to 63.4 percent to 92.5 percent. In India, the decline in manufacturing, especially in textiles, was sparked by a wide range of factors. The consolidation of rule under the British, for example, shrank markets associated with the multiple royal courts that had divided India before the nineteenth century. At the same time, British control of customs and tariffs both at home and on the subcontinent allowed British textiles to flood the Indian market while pricing better quality Indian goods out of the British market. The British also altered India's internal market with public works schemes that stimulated greater demand for coarser British cloth among the lower castes, while enhancing their ability to reach more distant areas thanks to the railroads constructed in mid-century. Finally, the British put a great deal of effort into studying Indian designs and techniques, for Indian cloth was highly valued throughout the world. Only after copying Indian practices while reducing the price, for example, was Britain able to capture the textile market in the Ottoman empire in the 1850s. Of course, a commitment to world trade was a double-edged sword, especially when it pitted industrial powers against one another. Later, when inexpensive Japanese silk entered the market in the early twentieth century, both Indian and British shares of the market fell. By that time, the British economy was better able to absorb the shock, but Indian weavers once again suffered. Since textiles represented a significant portion of manufacturing well into the nineteenth century throughout the world, the ability of industrial nations to damage the spinning and weaving industries in places like India, the Ottoman empire, and China meant not only that those who remained in the craft had to accept lower standards of living in order to compete, but also that thousands would have to leave the profession, resulting in dramatic economic restructuring.

Once states and traditional economies had been decimated, imperialist powers then set about remaking foreign economies to suit their needs. These new economic systems generated high rates of both structural and conjunctural poverty, while leaving societies increasingly vulnerable as populations continued to grow and stretch beyond available resources. In some areas, like Latin America and parts of sub-Saharan Africa and Southeast Asia, the extraction of raw materials, both crops and minerals, became the mainstay of the economy. These export-driven systems attracted a great deal of capital from foreign investors and increased the overall productivity of these regions, giving the impression of economic growth per capita, but such appearances are deceptive. They hide tremendous income disparities, for the elites who operated these mines and estates maximized their profits by enforcing coercive labor patterns. Although outright slavery had ceased to be an option in much of the world once Western nations devoted their energies to ending the slave trade in the mid-nineteenth century, its replacement in many areas, debt peonage, was hardly better. This was a form of indentured servitude fostered by paying laborers in advance and forcing them to shop in "company stores" that charged exorbitant prices. Once indebted, the workers had no choice but to submit to low wages with no prospect of seeking other employment until the debt was paid—a virtual impossibility. Structural poverty became their lot in life. Even if they did manage to pay their debts, the growth of towns and cities stripped the countryside of practically all occupations outside of agriculture, making it more difficult to survive by cobbling together an "economy of makeshifts." To escape this cycle of poverty, one had to migrate to the city. Unfortunately, life was little better in urban areas, where scholars write of "proletarianization" and persistent low wages as causes of widespread poverty. A study of housing in Nairobi conducted in the late 1930s, for instance, discovered almost 500 men, women, and children living in accommodations designed for no more than 163. As in industrial societies, such poverty was also more prevalent among women. In many sub-Saharan African cultures, agriculture and commerce were within the female purview, but imperialist powers now limited women's activity. Moreover, European control of education and large-scale enterprises restricted women's occupations and opportunities. Finally, in areas that experienced widespread seasonal or temporary migration based on employment opportunities in mines, on plantations, or in new urban areas, the groups left behind consisted primarily of women and children, who were often forced to scratch out a meager existence on available resources and the little that male workers succeeded in sending home.

At the same time, because these economies relied upon a world market for inexpensive raw materials, their societies as a whole remained extremely vulnerable to conjunctural poverty, especially if agriculture had switched over to monoculture, or the specialization in one cash crop. An abundant harvest, for instance, risked flooding the market. Lower profits meant not only a potential drop in wages for laborers, but also decreased spending and hard times for the merchants who supplied the needs of workers and elites. The entire economy could suffer, as happened in Brazil during the 1890s when the overproduction of coffee led to depressed world markets. In addition, because international coffee-trading companies controlled the market, they could afford to buy surpluses at low prices during harvest and then sell their stocks when the prices began to climb, preventing the profits from ever reaching Brazilian pocketbooks. That is why scholars refer to the Latin American economy as "neocolonial" during the nineteenth and twentieth centuries; economic power and control resided outside the hands of these nominally independent nations. In essence, the economic difficulties experienced by coffee planters in

Brazil differed little from those in the European colonies of East Africa. Conjunctural poverty also followed in the wake of the Great Depression of 1929, as crisis-stricken industrial economies dramatically cut back on their purchase of raw materials and agricultural commodities like coffee, sugar, and beef. In Latin America, the value of exports between 1930 and 1934 was only 48 percent of what it had been between 1925 and 1929. Meanwhile, sub-Saharan Africa experienced widespread unemployment for the first time in the 1930s. Despite plentiful resources, the continent's economy had been restructured to depend upon international markets, which could no longer support high demand. The Katanga copper mines in the Belgian Congo, for example, reduced their African workforce by over 60 percent between 1930 and 1933. At the same time, unemployment among able-bodied men reached 41 percent in Elizabethville (South Africa) and 25 percent in Nairobi (Kenya). In areas where monoculture had not yet become dominant, foodstuffs were still plentiful and relatively inexpensive, but this did little to alleviate the need for cash among the unemployed. In other areas, however, food was scarce, and attempts to diversify agriculture were hindered by the soil exhaustion caused by years of specialization in one main crop.

Even in areas less marked by dependence and large-scale farming and mineral extraction, imperialism spread impoverishment by encouraging widespread indebtedness. In some places, like the Ottoman empire, high taxes to pay the interest on foreign loans forced many peasants into sharecropping relationships based on cash advances for future harvests. While similar conditions, including a reorientation of agriculture to export markets, led to debt peonage and land concentration elsewhere, the availability of marginal land and the scarcity of labor, due to the high mortality from the empire's many wars during the nineteenth century, supported the proliferation of smallholdings among the Ottoman peasantry. In areas where landowners attempted to consolidate holdings and promote wage-labor on large estates, peasants either demanded high wages or migrated to areas where land was more available. In these conditions, elites decided that sharecropping was a more secure source of income. But the resulting low levels of productivity on small farms made it impossible for peasants to break out of debt, especially with usury rates running as high as 120 percent. Meanwhile, foreign competition with urban crafts made it impossible for poor peasants to seek opportunity in manufacturing. In the words of British envoy, Lewis Farley, in 1860:

> Turkey is no longer a manufacturing country. The numerous and varied manufactures which formerly sufficed, not only for the consumption of the empire, but which also stocked the markets of the Levant, as well as those of several countries in Europe, have in some instances, rapidly declined, and in others became altogether extinct. . . . There can be no doubt, therefore, entertained as to the possibility of an immense increase of the quantity of cotton grown in Turkey. . . . It is, in fact, this capability of supplying raw material at a low price and of excellent quality which gives to Turkish commerce that importance and consideration in which it is held by the European powers.

Unfortunately, that "importance and consideration" rested on the impoverishment of the Ottoman peasants, unable to plant and harvest enough to meet the overpowering burden of debt and taxes.

In many parts of China and India, smallholdings and sharecropping were also the norm, but this arose from overpopulation, not labor scarcity and an abundance of land. Between 1741 and 1850, the Chinese population grew 200 percent to 430 million people, but the amount of arable land grew by only 35 percent. While this alone led to peasant indebtedness, imperialism made conditions even worse. The outflow of silver initiated by the opium trade inflated the price of silver and skewed the silver/copper exchange system. In the eighteenth century, one tael of silver was worth 1,000 copper coins; by 1845 it was worth 2,000 copper coins. This hurt peasants who used copper as market currency, but had to pay taxes in silver. In essence, their tax burden doubled. Moreover, peasant tenants owed their rent in money, not in kind. And most landlords added property taxes to the rent, which could eventually reach as high as 60 percent of the crop yield. During the eighteenth century, many Chinese peasants were able to pay their bills only by participating in a thriving cottage industry, but this became more difficult in the nineteenth century, when competition from foreign goods destroyed cottage industry, first along the coasts and later, by the twentieth century, inland. While imperialist investment in the cities and concession areas gave rise to some employment opportunities, overpopulation kept wages low. The rise of the Guomindang (or Nationalist) government in the 1920s made some improvements in urban economic conditions, particularly once the Chinese government regained tariff autonomy by 1929 and began to recover concession areas in the 1930s, but this made little difference to the overwhelming majority of Chinese peasants, approximately 80 percent of the population, who languished in poverty in the countryside. According to a League of Nations study of South China, tenant and semi-tenant farming accounted for 60–90 percent of all agriculture, with occupants paying between 40 and 60 percent of the annual crop in rent. In this environment, structural poverty and indebtedness were so pervasive that traditional clan-based relief mechanisms began to break down.

Similar conditions developed in colonial India. However, the rise of smallholdings and widespread indebtedness arose more from what some historians describe as a "peasantization" of Indian society during the nineteenth century, when the decline of older internal market and bureaucratic centers led those who had once made their livings in commerce and crafts to turn to the land as the sole source of income. In the scramble for land, landlords began to raise rents and push more of the costs for upkeep onto the tenants. Meanwhile, as Indian capital no longer generated surpluses outside of agriculture, the economy soon mutated, leading Indian elites to emphasize squeezing the peasant economy as much as possible as a prime source of enrichment. Very little attention went to investment and entrepreneurialism. For their part, those who remained in urban crafts, like weavers who specialized in luxury cloth, were forced to lower both their standards of living and their own production costs in order to survive. The latter required them to purchase factory-made materials, like machine-spun yarn, which then increased their indebtedness to the middlemen who sold such commodities. Like sharecroppers, buying items necessary to production forced these craftsmen to borrow on the anticipated value of the finished product. One miscalculation in the price of either raw materials or completed merchandise could thus result in often debilitating debt. In the end, the Indian economy, like its Chinese and Ottoman counterparts, proved unable to stimulate the mass purchasing power that might have led to economic development, a situation that the Great Depression of 1929 only made worse. Instead, poverty became the norm.

Questions for Reflection

In this Perspectives excerpt, the author presents a much-needed global view of three related developments: industrialization, imperialism, and poverty. Does modern industrial society alleviate poverty or produce it? Politics has never been the same since this question was first posed by those witnessing this economic transformation first-hand. As you reflect on the quandary of industry's relationship to prosperity and poverty, then and now, answer the following questions.

1. Beaudoin argues that poverty beyond the borders of Western industrialized countries was no accident. Their policies made it so. "Imperialist powers destroyed traditional economic systems during the final decades of the nineteenth century and then set about creating new structures that better served their interests." According to the author, what principal strategies were involved in this process?

2. How did industrial powers go about recreating the traditional economies of colonized peoples? What parts of the world are noted in this context?

3. What role did debt play in creating dependent economies? What are some examples?

4. What is the point of the British envoy Lewis Farley's statement about Turkey?

5. In this excerpt, the author assumes a linkage between industrialization, imperialism, and poverty. What do you think of this linkage? What questions do you have about it?

6. This excerpt covers a lot of territory over many decades before and after WWI. In your view, which examples are most convincing and which are least persuasive?

7. Chronological reasoning, the ability to understand a complex sequence of events, is essential in the study of the past. How does the author's presentation on poverty in dependent economies rely on chronological reasoning?

8. After answering the questions above, what to you is left unanswered about the relationship between industrialization and poverty?

Activities Menu

Your instructor may assign one or more of the following learning activities:

Prewriting Exercise

Take a minute and write a paragraph (half page of notebook paper) on what you know about the origins of industrialization.

Media

Select a relevant video program from one of the following and write a one-page (double-spaced) reaction.

- TED Talk
- Munk Debates
- C-SPAN
- Crash Course

Source Search

Select and read two related primary sources found online at the Modern History Sourcebook and incorporate them into your discussion.

Class Discussion I

Use the questions above as the basis for a class discussion. Write out your answers ahead of time so that you will have plenty to say.

Class Discussion II

Select a handful of students and, using the questions above, debate the following statement: "The tragic irony of the age is that while industrialization is the most productive economic force in history, it has produced poverty along with prosperity."

Role-Playing Exercise

Explore the pros and cons of industrialization by assuming the role of one family in a working-class district of London or another European city. Tell us their story. Be descriptive. You will need to do a little research to pull this off. An excerpt from a Dickens novel might be of some help here.

Midterm Exam

Complete a midterm exam created by your instructor.

Suggested Reading

Steven M. Beaudoin, "Industrialization, Imperialism, and World Poverty, 1750-1945," in *Poverty in World History* (2007)

William D. Bowman, Frank M. Chiteji and J. Megan Greene, eds. *Imperialism in the Modern World: Sources and Interpretations* (2006)

Philip D. Curtain, *The World and the West: The European Challenge and the Overseas Response in the Age of Empire* (2002)

Laura L. Frader, *The Industrial Revolution: A History in Documents* (2006)

Emma Griffin, *Liberty's Dawn: A People's History of the Industrial Revolution* (2014)

PART II

<hr>

IN THE FINAL FOUR CHAPTERS of the book, we will reflect on a militant age, that of the late 19th, 20th, and early 21st centuries by considering the issues of war and the environment, individuals and history, ideology and power, and violence and the body politic. It seemed that despite its extraordinary advances in science, human rights, literature, and the arts, the Western world's other features—imperialism, world war, mass politics, social movements, global encounters, even its consumerism—possessed a militancy that forces us to count the costs of a journey that began when a few barely seaworthy ships set out on the world's oceans to span the distance between them and the rest of the world.

Chapter 5

Chapter Skill	Understanding Causation
Chapter Issue	War & the Environment
Chapter Objectives (Students will...)	• Identify three specific ways in which modern war impacted the environment • Assess two current perspectives on 20th century wars and their transformation of the global environment • Demonstrate in a discussion on war and the environment the ability to understand historical causation
Assignments and Assessments	1. Read the Setup Narrative 2. Listen to the Lecture(s) 3. Read the Perspectives excerpts 4. Take part in a role-playing Class Discussion

Setup Narrative: War & the Environment

Wars and those who start them bear responsibility for millions of human souls lost to the generations that sorely needed their presence, talents, and expertise. Just as precious is the earth that is, and forever will be, our only home. These conflicts, especially the world wars of the past century, marred and scarred our planet in ways we are just beginning to appreciate.

We should remind ourselves that these global conflicts began at a time that appeared to hold the promise of limitless progress. If we could go back in time and interview people in the late 19th century, we would hear stories of inventors whose breakthroughs in communications and travel, energy and electricity, and sanitation and urban planning almost guaranteed a better future. We would hear accounts of social reformers who tamed the lions of corporate and economic injustice through progressive legislation passed, be it said, by politicians like Theodore Roosevelt whose own well-heeled backgrounds belied such aims. We might be captivated by unbelievable tales of colonial encounters in Africa or Asia that brought ideals of a more civilized world within reach. And we ourselves could likely have told deeply personal accounts of our immigrant forebears who made their way to Europe or North America in search of a life that they had been told was something akin to paradise.

Others were skeptical and would have scoffed at stories like this. They pointed to growing inequality, colonial conflict and crimes, and generally a West whose Enlightenment had produced a distinctly unenlightened set of prejudices about other peoples, other "races." We can't be certain about human progress, they argued. In fact, moderns suggested, we can't be certain about certainty itself. What we can be clear about, they argued, is we are governed by our irrational and unconscious selves. Just look around. Freud and Nietzsche in their way both argued that there's more to personality and society than meets the eye, and the sooner we get on with dealing with basic instincts the better. It augured a new, very murky world, one that declared war on the liberal order, the working method of the West since the late 18th century. As some of the leading lights of the West declared war on the liberal order, the leading powers of Europe declared war on each other, with consequences no one could have foreseen.

As Europe went to war in 1914, it did so armed to the teeth. Its economy had been industrialized, and so had its militaries, which soon extended their influence over politics, too. The militarism of the early years of the 20th century gripped the West for the rest of the century. Its first victim was a set of defensive alliances that were supposed to prevent a wider war. In response to an assassination in the explosive tinderbox of southern Europe, the gears of those alliances were set in motion, which made a wider war a foregone conclusion for the belligerent — and related—monarchs of Europe. Carried along by a rising tide of nationalism, they were eager to fight, ready to rumble, and the parades and popular gatherings of the time whipped up an exalted war fever that pit the center of the continent (Germany, Austria-Hungary, Italy) against the Western and Eastern peripheries (Britain, France, and Russia). Convinced that any clash of this sort would be decisively concluded by Christmas, armies mobilized and set off for fronts that were soon locked in stalemate. Units dug in, literally, for a long fight that lasted nearly five Christmases, took 13 million lives, brought down four empires (the German, the Austro-Hungarian, the Ottoman, and the Russian), and devastated a whole generation. Partly because the Treaty of Versailles was intended to eliminate all future threats from Germany, the war to end all wars made another more likely. Both wars were global in scope, and both devastated the terrain of one of the most productive and scenic zones on the planet.

The human toll of the world wars has preoccupied us ever since, and rightly so, but what about the environmental toll? French farmers were still running across unexploded munitions from WWI into the 1990s. This and other legacies cause us to ponder a number of questions. What was trench warfare really like? What did this scar that ran from the Belgian coast to the Swiss border do to Europe? What were the environmental consequences of the world wars? Are we still coping with them in ways we don't fully understand? We are, and the excerpts below remind us that our mad bent to destroy ourselves in the 20th century eventually brought us back to earth, the very earth we depend upon for survival.

Lecture
Pay attention to the chapter lecture(s), either online or in class.

Tips on Understanding Causation

+ Remember not to confuse correlation with causation. Think about that.
+ Know not just what happened but why. In this chapter, that means being able to connect the dots carefully between local battles and the proximate environmental damage.
+ This is where it may be easier for us to see causes than contemporaries. Their primary sources are invaluable to us, but we may be able to see the big picture in a way they couldn't. When it comes to causation, time is on your side.

Environments of Death:
Trench Warfare on the Western Front, 1914–1918

by Dorothee Brantz

BELLIGERENT ENVIRONMENTS

Enemy fire was not the only wartime threat. Front-line soldiers also had to deal with changing weather conditions. Each season brought its own set of hazards that affected the day-to-day conduct of war—snow and freezing temperatures in the winter; heat, mosquitoes, and stench in the summer. On occasion, some soldiers even seemed to prefer combat to being exposed to the weather. For example, in early 1915, one French soldier wrote: "We don't think of death, but it's the cold, the terrible cold! It seems to me at the moment that my blood is full of blocks of ice. Oh, I wish they'd attack, because that would warm us up a little."[1] Soldiers in the opposing trenches expressed the same sentiment. Christian Krull, for example, noted, "We could not sleep because of all the vermin, wet, and cold. We went to the artillery gun and replaced the deadly tired gunners just so that we could get warm."[2] When it came to enduring these environmental conditions, all nations suffered equally.

One of the biggest problems, however, was the incessant rainfall that transformed the front into a sea of mud. It was one of the complaints soldiers voiced most often in their letters and in the front-line press. Describing the first day of June 1916, the French trench paper *L'Argonnaute* reported, "It has been raining all day, that cold, fine, relentless winter rain, against which there is no protection. The front-line trench is a mud-colored stream, but an unmoving stream where the current clings to the banks of its course. Water mud. You go down into it, you slip in gently, drawn in by who knows what irresistible force. ... Everything disappears into this ponderous liquid: men would disappear into it too if it were deeper."[3] Sometimes, the rain was so severe

Dorothee Brantz, "Environments of Death: Trench Warfare on the Western Front, 1914-1918," *War and the Environment: Military Destruction in the Modern Age,* ed. Charles E. Closmann, pp. 78-84, 89-91. Copyright © 2009 by Texas A&M University Press. Reprinted with permission.

that "though we were well aware of the shells, we really thought only of the rain. Inexhaustible clouds dumped an almost incessant downpour on the underbrush. The clay soil held the water on its surface. Our trenches were a brook, the woodland roads were lakes of mud, and the ditches alongside were tumbling torrents of a yellowish flood."[4] Indeed, during heavy downpours soldiers spent much of their time pumping water and mud out of the trenches. At times, torrential rains actually affected battles. For example, January 2, 1915, was apparently such a "dreadful day of rain, everything is so hazy that one cannot think about shooting."[5] Fog and continuous rainfall delayed the start of the Battle of Verdun for nine days.[6]

In addition to rain, mud became a chronic nuisance. In the words of one British soldier: "The memory of that [i.e., the western front] is mainly—mud."[7] Marc Bloch even referred to World War I as "the age of mud."[8] The chalky soil of Flanders and northern France had been easy to dig out, but "when the rain came in autumn, the trenches disappeared and the area became a lake of mud."[9] After days of rain, soldiers found that, "When we reach the communication trench, it is no longer a trench at all but a stream of fluid mud, where we sink over our leggings. We have to use our hands to pull out our legs when they get stuck."[10] And mud was not just unpleasant; it contributed to the hazards of front life. For example, one British soldier complained, "the mud on my greatcoat made it monstrously heavy, so that it flapped like lead against my legs, making the going utterly wearisome. I would willingly have died just then."[11] According to a March 1917 article in the French trench newspaper *Le Bochophage*, "mud throws its poisonous slobber out at him, closes around him, buries him. ... For men die of mud, as they die of bullets, but more horribly. Mud is where men sink and—what is worse—where their souls sink."[12] Some even compared the mud to an "enormous octopus" that swallowed men up, insisting, "hell is not fire, that would not be the ultimate in suffering. Hell is mud!"[13]

Another harrowing aspect of daily life in the trenches was the constant presence of vermin, most notably lice and rats. Weather conditions and vermin had always been a part of war to some degree. Whereas rain and mud underscored the continuous impact of weather, vermin pointed to the environmental consequences of stalemate warfare, which offered favorable conditions for the rats and lice that fed off human bodies, debris, and food supplies. The omnipresent vermin intensified soldiers' everyday misery, heightening the sense that civilization was coming to an end. One French trench paper described the situation as follows: "We would be thrilled not to find our bread contaminated by rats and our shirts invaded by vermin. If someone says, 'the *boches* are 20 meters away,' we feel a chill; but if we are told: 'the dug-outs are full of lice'—that we find really disgusting!"[14] Soldiers spent much of their time "chatting," mainly because to chat, at least in British parlance, meant to pick lice out of one's uniform (a "chat" was a louse); it proved to be a rather futile task, however, since it was ridiculous to kill an individual louse if one had hundreds of them.[15]

Whereas lice clung to soldiers' bodies, rats infested their surroundings. For rats, the trenches provided ideal habitats in which food was abundant and natural enemies were scarce (apart from soldiers and their rat-fighting pets). Feeding on food rations and the corpses of dead humans and animals, rats thrived and multiplied at an astonishing rate. Oddly enough, enemy fire was one of the few things that kept rat populations in check. Soldiers frequently reported how armies of rats fled areas where a grenade had hit.[16] Gas, too, tended to create panic among rat populations, which often served as early warning of an impending attack. A lieutenant colonel in the London Regiment at the Somme described a ghastly scene where, in the aftermath of a gas attack, "The trenches swarmed with rats, big rats, small rats, grey rats, tall rats in every stage of gas poisoning! Some were scurrying along scarcely affected while others were slowly dragging themselves about trying to find a corner in which to die. A most horrid sight—but a very good riddance."[17]

Apart from adding to the repulsive nature of life at the front, vermin also posed direct threats to soldiers' health. For example, just before the war, scientists had discovered that lice spread the bacterium that causes typhus, a highly lethal contagious disease that debilitated thousands of front-line soldiers and killed a fourth of those afflicted.[18] Rats also carried diseases that could be spread to humans. In general, the damp conditions coupled with poor hygiene in confined spaces increased soldiers' susceptibility to viral and bacterial infections of all kinds. The French army alone recorded close to five million cases of contagious disease between 1914 and 1918.[19] Even though World War I was the first military conflict in which more casualties were caused by weapons than disease, epidemics and other ailments continued to be a significant threat.[20] An ailment specific to World War I was trench foot, which occurred due to "prolonged standing in cold water or mud and by the continued wearing of wet socks, boots, and putters."[21] Even more perilous was the emergence of a new form of trench fever, which was first diagnosed in 1915.[22] Here, too, the louse proved to be the main vector, although its role in transmission was not established until after the war. To make matters worse, in 1917 influenza began to spread at the front, affecting 708,306 men on the German side alone between August 1917 and July 1918.[23] By that time, however, disease was far from the greatest threat to soldiers at the front.

On April 22, 1915, the Germans had launched the first successful chemical-weapons attack of the war, deploying more than 160 tons of chlorine gas at the Second Battle of Ypres.[24] This event marked a turning point in the history of military technology and inaugurated a type of warfare in which the environment itself could become a lethal weapon.[25] Conventional methods of combat were no longer the only or even the most efficient ways to wage war. Instead of penetrating the enemy's body with bombs, bullets, or blades, poison gas destroyed an adversary from the inside out.

Over the course of the war, all sides resorted to the use of poison gas. The British began using chlorine gas by September 1915, and by the end of the war, they had conducted 768 gas attacks discharging 57,000 tons of gas.[26] The number of gas shells rose from 1 percent of all fired shells in 1916 to 30 percent by 1918 in some sectors of the front.[27] The primary purpose of using gas was to terrorize the enemy. At first, gas was mainly utilized to initiate an attack, but with the arrival of chlorine shells, gas became a deadly weapon of attack that unleashed its yellow or greenish clouds over enemy trenches, blinding and suffocating soldiers en masse. As the French trench paper *Le Filou* stated: "We had seen everything: mines, shells, tear-gas, woodland demolished, the black tearing mines falling in fours, the most terrible wounds and the most murderous avalanches of metal—but nothing can compare with this fog which for hours that felt like centuries hid from our eyes the sunlight, the daylight, the clear whiteness of the snow."[28] In a similar vein, a British doctor remarked:

I shall never forget the sights I saw up by Ypres after the first gas attack. Men lying all along the side of the road between Poperinge and Ypres, exhausted, gasping, frothing yellow mucus from their mouths, their faces blue and distressed. It was dreadful and so little could be done for them. One came away from seeing or treating them longing to be able to go straight away at the Germans and to throttle them, to pay them out in some sort of way for their devilishness. Better for a sudden death than this awful agony.[29]

Gas was harmful not only to humans; it adversely affected every living creature. As *Le Filou* reported on March 20, 1917: "Little birds fell into the trenches, cats and dogs, our companions in misfortune, lay down at our feet and did not awaken."[30] Ernst Jünger, too, recalled how, after a gas attack, "A large number of plants were wilted, snails and moles were lying dead, and the messenger horses that were stabled in Monchy had water running out of their eyes and mouths."[31]

Gas represented a new weapons technology that did not kill directly but altered the environment in such a way as to make it uninhabitable. In order to comprehend the full extent of the devastation caused by World War I, we must recognize that machine-age warfare was not simply the result of other technological means to kill people but also of incorporating the environment into this destruction. In other words, when thinking about the place of the environment in warfare, we should think of it not merely as a stage for combat but as a constitutive element of warfare that directly influenced the course of battles. For one, weapons functioned only if the environment cooperated. In World War I this was often not the case, as was shown by, for example, the inability of tanks—another innovation of this war—to move through the cratered fields of mud. Hence, neither environment nor weaponry can be viewed as completely separate entities because both were interdependent in the age of total warfare (Figure 4.1).

World War I required a new synergy not just between man and machines but also between technology and the environment, including animals. During World War I the interrelationship of weaponry and the environment reached an unprecedented level in the sense that innovations in military technology, particularly heavy artillery and poison gas, led to a type of destruction that no longer focused exclusively on the killing of soldiers but instead aimed at the indiscriminate and total annihilation of everything. It was modern technology that made possible the mass slaughters that characterize twentieth-century warfare.

CONCLUSION

By November 1918, four million of the approximately thirty-two million men in uniform had been killed, and millions more had been permanently disabled or disfigured.[32] At the Battle of the Somme alone, France lost every third soldier of the 1.5 million they had sent in. Of the 2.5 million Germans, 700,000 became casualties of war. The British army lost more men in these three months than during the entirety of World War II.[33] In addition to the human death toll, millions of animals were killed in this stalemate slaughter.

Villages and towns lay in ruins, fields had been turned into moonscapes, and forests had been reduced to acres of stumps (Figure 4.2). The French Forestry Service estimated that 350,000 hectares of forest had been destroyed during the war, an amount that would have supplied the

FIGURE. 4.1 Devastated landscape near Ypres with disabled British Mark IV tank, 1917. Unknown photographer. © Bildarchiv Preußischer Kulturbesitz.

tree harvest for the next sixty years.[34] As the writer Arnold Zweig describes it: "Beautiful villages first became ruins, then mounds of rubble, and finally stretches of bricks; woods first [became] gaps and tangles, then fields of dead pale stumps, eventually desert."[35]

The conflict had also unsettled existing notions of landscape and property relations, imposing its own set of war-specific environmental conditions, which grew out of the intended and unintended consequences of military destruction. The western front gave rise to a distinct environment of trenches and no-man's-land filled with the intense sounds, sights, and smells of a war of attrition bent on the massive destruction of human lives as well as nature. Indeed, symbolically the death of soldiers was closely tied to the death of nature. One manifestation of this connection between soldiers and nature was the commemoration of the dead. Describing the German *Heldenhaine,* George Mosse wrote: "Nature itself was supposed to serve as a living monument; the German forest provided a fitting environment for the cult of the fallen soldier."[36]

War created a new *Schicksalsgemeinschaft* (community of fate) between men and nature, who threatened each other in the daily practice of warfare, but who also amalgamated into a new symbolic unity born out of their mutual annihilation. According to Ernst Toller, "A forest is a Volk. A shot-up forest is an assassinated Volk."[37] Even more tellingly, another German soldier wrote: "The fate of this forest is linked and interwoven with my own at the deepest level. Not only were the woods my comrade but also my protection, a shield that wards off the lead and iron hurled at me ... allowing itself be pierced to the heart; it yields to death without resistance

FIGURE. 4.2 Tree ravaged by artillery fire, 1915. Postcard, unknown photographer. Courtesy of the Mauch and Roller families, Weil im Schönbuch, Germany.

so that I may live. Often when thick clouds have obscured the sun ... [and] the day is full of melancholy and sadness, then bright drops trickle from the trees' flayed crowns like tears of never-ending pain."[38]

Notes
1. Entry dated January 19, 1915, in Roger Campana, *Les enfants de la "Grande Revanche": Carnet de route d'un Saint-Cyrien, 1914–1918* (Paris, 1920), 69; quoted here from Eksteins, *Rites of Spring*, 148.

2. "Vor Ungeziefern und Nässe und Kälte konnten wir nicht schlafen, stürzten ans Geschütz und lösten die todmüden Kanoniere ab, nur dass wir warm wurden." Letter from Christian Krull dated July 29, 1916, quoted here from Ulrich and Ziemann, eds., *Frontalltag im Ersten Weltkrieg*, 92.

3. *L'Argonnaute*, June 1, 1916, in Stéphane Audoin-Rouzeau, *Men at War, 1914–1918: National Sentiment and Trench Journalism in France during the First World War*, trans. Helen McPhail (Providence and Oxford: Berg, 1992), 38.

4. Bloch, *Memoirs of War*, 102.

5. "[H]eute ist ein abscheulicher Regentag; es ist alles so verschleiert, daß an Schießen nicht zu denken ist." Marc, *Briefe aus dem Feld*, 45.

6. The Battle of Verdun was supposed to have started on February 10, 1916, but did not commence until February 19. On the role of the weather during the battle's first weeks, see, among others, Alain Denizot, "Combattre à Verdun," in Carlier and Pedroncini, eds., *La Bataille de Verdun*, 33; Neitzel, *Blut und Eisen*, 85; and Robin Neillands, *Attrition: The Great War on the Western Front, 1916* (London: Robson, 2001), 77.

7. A. A. Dickson, "Varieties of Trench Life," in *True World War I Stories*, 186.

8. Bloch, *Memoirs of War*, 152.

9. Frank Watson, "A Territorial in the Salient," in *True World War I Stories*, 27.

10. Lafond, *Covered with Mud and Glory*, 221.

11. W. Walker, "The Battle of Loos," *True World War I Stories*, 39.

12. Smith, Audoin-Rouzeau, and Becker, *France and the Great War*, 89.

13. *Le Bochophage*, March 26, 1917, quoted here from Audoin-Rouzeau, *Men at War*, 38.

14. *Le Pépère*, April 21, 1916, quoted here from ibid., 42.

15. Ashworth, *Trench Warfare*, 5.

16. Maze, *Frenchman in Khaki*, 242, cited in Habeck, "Die Technik im Ersten Weltkrieg—von unten gesehen," 117.

17. Letter by Lt. Col. Sir Robert Tolerton to his fiancée on July 10, 1916, reprinted in Richter, *Chemical Soldiers*, 137.

18. Edmund Russell, *War and Nature: Fighting Humans and Insects with Chemicals from World War I to Silent Spring* (New York: Cambridge University Press, 2001), 26; and Paul Weindling, "The First World War and the Campaigns against Lice: Comparing British and German Sanitary Measures," in *Die Medizin und der Erste Weltkrieg*, ed. Wolfgang Eckart and Christoph Gradmann (Pfaffenweiler: Centaurus, 1996), 227.

19. Audoin-Rouzeau and Becker, *France and the Great War*, 89.

20. In 1916, Friedrich Prinzing published his internationally acclaimed work *Epidemics Resulting from Wars* (Oxford: Clarendon, 1916), in which he outlined some of the major epidemics that threatened front-line soldiers.

21. *Notes for Infantry Officers on Trench Warfare*, 53.

22. Major J. Graham, "Trenchfever," *Lancet* (September 25, 1915).

23. Gerhard Hirschfeld, Gerd Krumeich, and Irina Renz, eds. *Enzyklopädie Erster Weltkrieg* (Paderborn: Schöningh, 2004), 460. See also Jürgen Müller, "Die Spanische Influenza 1918/19: Einflüsse des Ersten Weltkrieges auf Ausbreitung, Krankheitsverlauf und Perzeption einer Pandemie," in Eckart and Gradmann, eds., *Die Medizin und der Erste Weltkrieg*, 321–42.

24. Gas had first been used by the French police in 1912. See Chrisoph Gradmann, "'Vornehmlich beängstigend': Medizin, Gesundheit und chemische Kriegführung im deutschen Herr 1914-1918," in Eckart and Gradmann, eds., *Die Medizin und der Erste Weltkrieg*, 131–54; Rolf-Dieter Müller, "Total War as a Result of New Weapons? The Use of Chemical Agents in World War I," in Chickering and Förster, eds., *Great War, Total War: Combat and Mobilization on the*

Western Front, 1914–1918, 95–111. On the use of poison gas in World War I, see also Ludwig Fritz Haber, *The Poisonous Cloud: Chemical Warfare in the First World War* (Oxford: Clarendon Press, 1986); Olivier Lepick, *La Grande Guerre chimique: 1914–1918* (Paris: Presses universitaires de France, 1998); Dieter Martinetz, *Der Gaskrieg 1914/18: Entwicklung, Herstellung und Einsatz chemischer Kampfstoffe, das Zusammenwirken von militärischer Führung, Wissenschaft und Industrie* (Bonn: Bernard and Graefe, 1996); Donald Richter, *Chemical Soldiers: British Gas Warfare in World War I* (Lawrence: University Press of Kansas, 1992); and Ulrich Trumpener, "The Road to Ypres: The Beginnings of Gas Warfare in World War I," *Journal of Modern History* 47 (1975): 460–80.

25. Four types of gases were used in World War I: lacrimators or "tear gases" such as benzyl bromide; sternutators or vomiting gases; lung irritants such as chlorine, phosgene and carbon oxychloride; and skin irritants such as mustard gas.

26. Neillands, *Attrition,* 98; and Richter, *Chemical Soldiers,* 228.

27. Müller, "Total War as a Result of New Weapons," 101. *Environments of Death* 91

28. Audoin-Rouzeau, *Men at War,* 72.

29. Lt. Col. G. W. G. Hughes in April 1915, cited in Richter, *Chemical Soldiers,* 6.

30. Audoin-Rouzeau, *Men at War,* 72.

31. "Ein großer Teil aller Pflanzen war verwelkt, Schnecken und Maulwürfe lagen tot umher, und den in Monchy untergebrachten Pferden der Meldereiter lief das Wasser aus Maul und Augen." Jünger, *In Stahlgewittern,* 90.

32. Ellis and Cox, *The World War I Data Book,* 269–70. See also Denis Winter, *Death's Men: Soldiers of the Great War* (London: Viking, 1978), 251–54.

33. Michael Salewski, *Der Erste Weltkrieg* (Paderborn: Schöningh, 2003), 207.

34. John Jeanneney, "The Impact of World War I on French Timber Resources," *Journal of Forest History* 22 no. 4 (October 1978): 226–27, esp. 226.

35. "Die schönen Dörfer waren erst Ruinen geworden, dann Trümmerhaufen, schließlich Ziegelstätten; die Wälder erst Lücken und Knäuel, dann Leichenfelder bleicher Stümpfe, schließlich Wüste." Arnold Zweig, *Erziehung vor Verdun* (Leipzig: P. Reclam, 1971), 101.

36. Mosse, *Fallen Soldiers,* 109.

37. "Ein Wald ist ein Volk. Ein zerschossener Wald ist ein gemeucheltes Volk." Ernst Toller, *Eine Jugend in Deutschland,* vol. 4 of Ernst Toller, *Gesammelte Werke,* ed. John M. Spalek and Wolfgang Frühwald, 5 vols. (Munich: Hanser, 1978), 64.

38. "Das Schicksal dieses Waldes ist mit dem meinigen aufs innigste verquickt und verworben. Nicht nur Kamerad ist mir der Wald geworden, sondern auch starker Schutz; ein Schild, der das gegen mich geschleuderte tödliche Blei und Eisen abwendet … sich ins Herz bohren läßt; sich selbst wehrlos dem Tode beugt, auf das ich lebe. Oft wenn dicke Wolken die Sonne verdrängt haben … der Tag erfüllt ist von Wehmut und Trauer, dann perlen die hellen Tropfen aus den zerschundenen Kronen, wie Tränen eines unendlichen Schmerzes." H. O. Rehlke, "Der gemordete Wald," in *Die Feldgraue Illustrierte: Kriegszeitschrift der 50. Infantrie Division* (June 1916), 12.

The Global Environmental Footprint of the U.S. Military, 1789–2003

by J.R. McNeill and David S. Painter

MILITARY INFRASTRUCTURE AND THE ENVIRONMENT SINCE 1941

Both the size and power of the U.S. military escalated tremendously during World War II. Although the level of the U.S. armed forces dropped sharply from 12.1 million in 1945 to 1.7 million by mid-1947, the United States still possessed the world's most powerful military machine in the ensuing years. The U.S. Navy, bolstered by wartime shipbuilding, controlled the seas; U.S. air power dominated the skies; and the United States alone possessed atomic weapons and the means to deliver them. Following the Soviet Union's acquisition of atomic weapons in 1949, the United States sought to maintain strategic superiority through increased production of atomic weapons and development of the hydrogen bomb (see below). The Korean War (1950–53) led to another massive increase in U.S. military spending, and the United States expanded its armed forces by over a million troops and sharply increased production of aircraft, ships, combat vehicles, and other conventional weapons. The U.S. nuclear arsenal also grew dramatically from roughly one thousand warheads in 1953 to approximately eighteen thousand by 1960. Although the United States began to reduce the size of its conventional forces and slow the rate of production of nuclear warheads in the 1970s, each new generation of weapons possessed more destructive power, consumed more energy, and had a greater environmental impact.

The experience of World War II changed the way the American public thought about national security interests and requirements. Drawing on what they believed to be the lessons of the 1930s, U.S. leaders sought to create and maintain a favorable balance of power in Europe and Asia, to fashion an international economic order open to U.S. trade and investment, and to maintain the integration of the third world in the world economy in an era of decolonization and national liberation. To achieve these goals, U.S. leaders considered a global network of military bases essential to national defense. These bases would also serve to deter aggression against American interests and to influence events abroad by projecting U.S. power into potential trouble spots. Maintaining nuclear superiority was also seen as a crucial element of national defense strategies, which included both preempting attacks on the United States and preventing Soviet advances elsewhere in the world. These policies were designed not only to ensure the physical security of the United States and its allies but also to preserve a broadly defined "American way of life" by constructing an international order that would be open to and compatible with U.S. interests and ideals.[1] Until the deployment of B-52 intercontinental bombers in the late 1950s and long-range land- and submarine-launched ballistic missiles in the 1960s, the U.S. nuclear deterrent was heavily dependent on bombers and ballistic missiles that could not reach the Soviet Union from the United States. Likewise, conventional forces needed to be close to potential theaters of conflict if they were to be able to influence events. These geographical and technological factors made the United States dependent on bases in the territories of its allies.

The United States developed an archipelago of military facilities around the world covering around 810,000 hectares or something over two million acres, making it nearly the size of Lebanon or Connecticut. By the mid-1960s the United States had approximately 375 major military bases in foreign countries and 3,000 minor military facilities spread around the world. The largest single concentration of U.S. troops was in Europe, and over two-thirds of these were in West Germany. There were also large concentrations of U.S. forces in Japan (including Okinawa), the Philippines, South Korea, and Great Britain. By the end of the Cold War there were more than 525,000 U.S. troops permanently based overseas. A decade later the number of U.S. troops deployed overseas had fallen to around 235,000, with 109,000 in Europe, 93,000 in Asia, and 23,000 in the Persian Gulf. In addition, the United States had increasingly begun to substitute the pre-positioning of equipment, munitions, and fuel for the overseas deployment of military manpower. This new policy became standard procedure in the Middle East, where the presence of large numbers of U.S. military personnel was a particularly sensitive issue.[2]

The size and nature of American forces abroad dramatically affected the ecosystems in and around overseas military bases, which were usually exempt from both local and U.S. environmental regulations. In addition to such special classes of lethal by-products as radioactive material, high explosives, chemical weapons, and rocket fuels, U.S. military bases generated massive amounts of hazardous wastes as part of their normal operations. The routine maintenance of the vast numbers of ships, aircraft, combat and support vehicles, and weaponry produced such pollutants as used oil and solvents, polychlorinated biphenyls (PCBs), battery and other acids, paint sludge, heavy metals, asbestos, cyanide, and plating residues. Sometimes the size of small cities, U.S. bases also produced large amounts of ordinary garbage, medical wastes, photographic chemicals, and sewage.[3] Often these wastes, toxic and nontoxic alike, were disposed of casually. In a 1991 study of seven U.S. bases in Europe and the Pacific, General Accounting Office inspectors discovered ground or water contamination at five of the seven bases and four of the six central waste-disposal facilities examined.[4]

Training and maneuvers altered local landscapes, consumed vast amounts of energy, and contributed to air pollution, including the carbon dioxide buildup in the atmosphere that is responsible for climate change. The amount of land required for military maneuvers has increased dramatically since World War II as the size, speed, and complexity of military weapons and equipment have grown. In addition to the obvious impact of gunnery and bombing exercises, which cause not only immediate damage but also long-term hazards due to unexploded ordnance, the effects of large numbers of heavy vehicles on the land could be devastating to soil, vegetation, and waterways.[5]

Some of the worst environmental damage occurred at U.S. bases in the Philippines and Panama. The two largest bases in the Philippines, Clark Air Base and Subic Bay Naval Base, covered more than 77,000 hectares (or upward of 190,270 acres) and served as rear areas during the Korean War and major staging areas for the U.S. war in Vietnam. They continued to play an important role in U.S. strategy in the 1970s and '80s as a link to the Indian Ocean and Persian Gulf and as a means of countering the expanded Soviet naval presence in Asia. Following extensive damage to Clark and Subic Bay by the eruption of Mt. Pinatubo in 1991, the Philippine Senate refused to renew its agreement with the United States, leading to closure of these bases. More than four decades' worth of operations at the Clark and Subic Bay bases had generated huge amounts of hazardous waste, much of which was dumped into open drains or buried in unprotected land-fills. Moreover, leakage from underground petroleum tanks and from the petroleum pipeline connecting Subic Bay to Clark Air Base had contaminated local groundwater, and unexploded ordnance continued to claim Filipino victims long after the U.S. military's departure.[6]

During World War II the U.S. base system in Panama developed into one of the world's greatest concentrations of American military force overseas, peaking at 63,000 troops in 1943. While the Canal facilitated the deployment of U.S. naval forces during World War II, postwar aircraft carriers were too large to pass through the locks, and the role of U.S. forces in Panama shifted from enhancing the nation's global reach to maintaining U.S. influence in Latin America. By the 1970s there were eleven major U.S. military installations in Panama. The 1977 Panama Canal treaties not only returned control of the canal to Panama by the end of the century but also required the withdrawal of the U.S. military presence. In July 1999 the Southern Command moved to Miami and Puerto Rico, and in December of that year the United States turned over its last military bases in Panama.

During World War II the U.S. military conducted numerous tests of chemical weapons in Panama, especially on San José Island in Panama Bay, which acquired the nickname "Test-Tube Island." After the war, the military continued to store and experiment with chemical weapons in Panama, including environmental tests of sarin and VX nerve gas, which sought to determine the effects of storage in tropical conditions on these deadly agents. The military also tested the dangerous defoliant Agent Orange in Panama and stored and tested depleted uranium munitions.[7] In addition to storing, testing, and disposing of chemical weapons in several areas of the country, the U.S. military maintained several firing ranges in Panama. According to one estimate, "the United States left more than one hundred thousand pieces of unexploded ordnance in Panama."[8]

Despite the scale of the overseas bases, the environmental damage caused by the U.S. military was greater at home than abroad. Less than a fifth of U.S. military manpower was stationed overseas, so the main impact has been within the fifty states, where by the end of the Cold War the Department of Defense directly controlled over ten million hectares of land (close to twenty-five million acres) and leased another 80,000 hectares (more than 197,000 acres) from other federal agencies. The Department of Energy, which is responsible for the production of nuclear weapons, also controlled around 10,000 hectares (approximately 24,710 acres). Many of the same problems that existed at bases overseas affected the environment within the United States. In 1993 the Department of Defense listed more than 19,000 contaminated sites in over 1,700 active military facilities across the country. Although portions of these vast holdings have suffered extensive and lasting damage, some areas have been spared the environmental disruption that accompanies commercial development, their presumable fate had they not been controlled by the military.[9]

Much of the environmental destruction wrought by the military during the twentieth century has been connected to the use of oil-fueled weapons systems and transport vehicles, including naval vessels and aircraft. Although the navies of the United States and the great European powers played a relatively minor role in World War I, oil and the internal combustion engine heralded a revolution in mobility on land, sea, and in the air. Oil was also used in the manufacture of munitions and synthetic rubber.[10]

Although the development of nuclear weapons and ballistic missiles and, more recently, the integration of computer technology into weapons systems have fundamentally altered the nature of warfare, oil remains vital to U.S. military power. Each new generation of weapons has also required more oil than its predecessor. For example, according to one estimate, a U.S. armored division in World War II consumed about 60,000 gallons of gasoline daily.[11] In contrast, a 2001 Defense Science Board study estimates that an armored division requires ten times that amount of fuel per day.[12]

During the Cold War the need to ensure sufficient supplies of oil for U.S. forces in Europe led to the creation of the Central European Pipeline System (CEPS), one of the most complex and extensive pipeline systems in the world. Running from the Atlantic and Mediterranean coasts of France to Heidelberg and Amsterdam, the CEPS included over fifty depots, nearly thirty pumping stations, and close to 6,000 kilometers of buried pipeline.[13] In one case, jet fuel leaked from underground pipelines at the Rhein-Main Air Base in Germany and contaminated the underground aquifer supplying water to the city of Frankfurt.[14] There were also shorter pipelines in other European countries. For example, in the 1950s the United States built a seven-hundred-kilometer-long petroleum pipeline connecting its naval base in Rota, Spain, with airfields at Moron, Torrejon, and Zaragoza because, as one analyst noted, "a wing of B-47s (medium-range bombers) consumes in an afternoon more fuel than the entire Spanish railroad tanker fleet can transport in a month."[15]

TABLE 5.1 Energy consumption of selected U.S. military equipment

Equipment	Operating Distance or Time	Fuel Consumption (in liters)
M-1 Abrams Tank, average use	1 kilometer	47
F-15 jet, at peak thrust	1 minute	908
M-1 Abrams Tank, peak rate	1 hour	1,113
F-4 Phantom fighter/bomber	1 hour	6,359
Battleship	1 hour	10,810
B-52 bomber	1 hour	13,671
Non-nuclear aircraft carrier	1 hour	21,300
Carrier battle group	1 day	1,589,700
Armored division (348 tanks)	1 day	2,271,000

Although the U.S. military shrank somewhat in size following the end of the Cold War, it still maintained more than 150,000 ground vehicles, 22,000 aircraft, and hundreds of oceangoing vessels.[16] This fleet guaranteed that conventional military operations would be an oil-intensive activity (see Table 5.1). Indeed, maintaining access to oil has become a top priority for the U.S. military. It is currently the single largest consumer of petroleum products in the world and a major contributor to global carbon emissions. Even excluding the additional fuel demands of the Gulf War (1991) and the Serbia-Kosovo bombing campaigns (1999), the U.S. military's annual energy consumption during the 1990s was greater than the total commercial energy consumption of nearly two-thirds of the world's countries.[17] For fiscal year 2003 the Defense Energy Support Center—the agency that manages the military's oil supply—made arrangements to purchase around 184 million barrels of petroleum products. Jet fuels made up 73.5 percent of the total, followed by ground fuels (18.6 percent) and marine fuels (7.93 percent).[18]

According to one estimate, the U.S. military at the end of the Cold War accounted directly for around 2 to 3 percent of total U.S. energy demand and 3 to 4 percent of oil demand, including almost 27 percent of the nation's total consumption of jet fuel. These figures do not include the energy used in manufacturing weapons. Moreover, the military's share of total U.S. use of nonfuel minerals ranged from 5 to 15 percent, and mining operations to extract these minerals often caused significant environmental damage.[19]

In addition to the direct impact of military activities on the environment, numerous indirect effects included new economic and settlement patterns, higher energy consumption, and a greater reliance on private transit. During World War II, U.S. defense spending determined the location of much of the nation's industrial activity and thus had a major influence on its economic geography and population patterns. The U.S. military budget fell between 1945 and 1950 but rose sharply during the Korean War, reaching 12.7 percent of the Gross National Product (GNP) in 1954 and averaging around 5 percent of the GNP from 1950 through 1990. As a result, highly specialized enclaves devoted to military production arose in California, Colorado, the Pacific Northwest, New England, and the South, a development that hastened the decline of the old industrial heartland stretching from New York to Michigan. These economic and demographic shifts left a significant human footprint in terms of roads, buildings, and water use in the South and West.[20]

National-security arguments provided political support for the U.S. Interstate Highway System, first conceived in 1944 and approved by Congress in 1956. Between 1956 and 1970 the federal government spent around $70 billion on the 68,000-kilometer (42,000-mile) National System of Interstate and Defense Highways linking the country's major population centers. During the same period the federal government spent $795,000 on rail transit.[21] The patterns of social and economic organization fostered by the U.S. military have resulted in the subsidization of private automobile use, the consequent deterioration of public transportation, and continuing population shift s to the suburbs as well as to the South and West, changes that have stimulated ever-higher levels of energy use. These have contributed greatly to carbon dioxide buildup, the proliferation of ambient lead (before lead was eliminated from gasoline in the United States in the 1980s), and other atmospheric pollution problems deriving from vehicle use.

Easily the most durable environmental effects of the American military will be those associated with the atomic weapons program: one of the radionuclides generated, plutonium-239, has a half-life of up to 480,000 years. In the United States, as elsewhere, the military built nuclear weapons to address immediate threats and gave scant consideration to the long-term consequences. The American program began in 1942 and by 1945 had bombs ready for use, two of which were dropped on Japan, bringing World War II to a close. Then, in the context of Cold War anxieties, the Americans expanded their nuclear arsenal and tested over a thousand weapons before agreeing to a moratorium on testing in 1993.

The tests, which involved deliberate releases of radiation into the environment, contaminated almost every corner of the country and the globe (although it is impossible to separate the effects of American atmospheric testing from those of the USSR, Britain, and France, which together tested roughly as many weapons as did the Americans). Most testing took place in sparsely populated desert regions (often on Shoshone Indian lands in Nevada), although the United States also tested hydrogen bombs on two Pacific atolls, leaving them devastated by blasts and dangerously contaminated for the foreseeable future. Testing killed a few thousand sheep in Nevada and probably killed a few thousand people indirectly, through cancers resulting from radiation exposure. But the epidemiology of cancer and its relation to radiation remains controversial, and little reliable data exists.

The longer-term effects are linked to the problem of nuclear waste. The atomic weapons program generated radioactive waste on thousands of sites across the country, most notably the bomb factories of the Hanford Engineering Works (in Washington State) and the Rocky Flats Arsenal (in Colorado). In the heat of Cold War tensions, the issue of waste management was left to future generations to resolve, so that containment of radioactive materials, of which there are millions of tons, was at first (until the 1970s) rather haphazard. Groundwater contamination is among the most immediate risks, especially around Hanford. Since the 1970s, and especially since the 1990s, the Department of Defense has undertaken cleanup efforts that ultimately will cost far more than was spent to build the weapons in question. But much of the mess can never be cleaned up: the United States, like other nuclear powers, blithely assumed a radioactive waste management obligation that will last tens of thousands, perhaps hundreds of thousands of years, a period of time far longer than states, civilizations, and even (in the case of plutonium-239) anatomically modern human beings have existed. Future historians will face a daunting task when they seek to explain to generations yet unborn the mentality that led authorities in the United States, and elsewhere, to create this burden.[22]

COMBAT AND THE ENVIRONMENT SINCE 1941

In comparison to the environmental effects of preparation for war, those of combat itself appear modest and fleeting. Since 1941, the U.S. military has fought a half-dozen genuine wars and involved itself in several additional smaller operations. We will briefly consider three of these conflicts: World War II, the Vietnam War, and the 1991 Gulf War.

In World War II the main theaters of operations for U.S. forces were North Africa, southern and western Europe, and the Pacific. The ground war in North Africa and Europe produced initially devastating environmental consequences, especially in cities, but that damage was repaired by patient labor within ten to twenty years. Tank warfare in the North African desert, which broke the sand crusts, led to more intense sandstorms for many decades.[23] Some of the Pacific islands that saw bitter fighting—Saipan, Iwo Jima, and Okinawa, for example—were almost entirely shorn of vegetation. But once combat ceased, patterns of ecological succession took hold, approximately as they do after a natural fire. On many atolls, U.S. forces built airstrip pavements out of coral, which destroyed local reefs at least temporarily. In some respects World War II combat brought a respite from ordinary peacetime environmental pressures. For example, the dangers of submarine warfare obliged fishing fleets to sit out the war in port, giving North Atlantic fisheries four years in which to flourish. (Oil spills from sinking tankers and depth charges posed a far smaller risk for fish than did fishermen.)

In Vietnam, where the Americans took over a colonial war from the French in the 1950s and committed forces heavily after 1964, the major environmental effects came from aerial attacks. American bombers put about twenty million craters in Vietnam (many of which now serve as fishponds), and the United States used chemical defoliants and herbicides on a large scale (a practice pioneered by the British in the Malayan insurgency of the 1950s) in attempts to remove the forest cover so vital to guerilla operations. This reduced the forest area of Vietnam by about 23 percent.[24] The defoliants also caused severe health problems for thousands of Vietnamese and for many American soldiers as well.[25]

In the case of the Gulf War, by far the most dramatic environmental damage was perpetrated in Kuwait by Iraqi forces, who ignited some seven hundred oil wells, causing fires that blackened the skies for months and lowered surface temperatures by about ten degrees centigrade. Intentional spills generated temporary oil rivers and lakes in Kuwait and contaminated 40 percent of the country's water supply, polluting it so thoroughly that it remains unusable. The spills also damaged the shorelines of the Persian Gulf for hundreds of kilometers, although with few apparent long-term effects—which in any case are now hard to distinguish from the harm caused by the oil spills that routinely occur in the Gulf and by earlier spills associated with the Iran–Iraq War of the 1980s.[26] The Iraqis also laid more than 1.5 million landmines in Kuwait. One way or another, almost a third of the surface area of the country was affected. The damage to desert and marine life was substantial. Fortunately Kuwait is a rich country and can afford to pay for environmental remediation—although there is none to be had at any price for the contaminated groundwater and some of the oil-soaked soils.[27]

For their part, the Americans sank numerous Iraqi oil tankers and bombed one oil terminal, adding to the marine spills. They also used armor-piercing shells of depleted uranium, which, upon hitting their targets (or anything else), released uranium oxide into the air. The health effects of this type of ordnance are much disputed, but it may be responsible for birth defects and pediatric cancers.[28] Iraq is not in a position to pay for much environmental remediation and has in any case other priorities—including, since 2003, another war that will surely leave its own environmental legacy.

CONCLUSION

Before the 1890s the environmental implications of the U.S. military hardly reached beyond the nation's borders, and its chief mission was to support settlement with all the ecological changes that process implied. But from the 1890s, the United States sought a larger role in world politics, and the ecological effects of its military establishment became increasingly global. That process began with the acquisition of overseas bases after 1898 and culminated in the post-1941 sprawling archipelago of bases and installations around the world.

The direct environmental impacts were mainly those associated with military bases at home and abroad, with their infrastructure, with their chemical and nuclear wastes, and with the disruptions caused by training and maneuvers—all of which was subject to minimal regulation, especially overseas. The military's fuel use alone was staggering; an F-16 fighter jet burned as much fuel in an hour as the average American motorist used in two years. Impacts even extended into space, because the American military was among the earliest and most prolific producers of "space junk," which includes discarded pieces of satellites, rocket boosters, and the like. Combat, too, had its effects on the environment, particularly in labile ecosystems such as those of deserts or small islands.

Beyond these direct effects, the military contributed to new efficiencies in American manufacturing in the nineteenth century, to new industries (chemical herbicides and pesticides) in the early twentieth century, to new settlement patterns in the United States after 1941, and to a way of life that involved unprecedented levels of energy use. The United States was of course not alone in recasting ecology at home and abroad while preparing for and fighting wars. It was unique only in the extent to which it did so, an extent that corresponded to the global reach of American military power over the past sixty years. The ambition to dominate world politics seemed to require that American society, not merely the U.S. military, seek to dominate nature as well.

Notes

1. Melvyn P. Leffler, *A Preponderance of Power: National Security, the Truman Administration, and the Cold War* (Stanford, Cal.: Stanford University Press, 1992).
2. In addition to Sandars, *America's Overseas Garrisons,* see Joseph Gerson and Bruce Bichard, eds., *The Sun Never Sets: Confronting the Network of U.S. Military Bases* (Boston: Beacon Press, 1991); Chalmers Johnson, *The Sorrows of Empire: Militarism, Secrecy, and the End of the Republic* (New York: Metropolitan Books, 2004).
3. U.S. General Accounting Office, *Hazardous Waste: Management Problems Continue at Overseas Military Bases,* Report to the Chairman, Subcommittee on Environment, Energy and Natural Resources, Committee on Government Operations, House of Representatives, GAO/NSIAD-91–231 (Washington, D.C.: Government Printing Office, 1991), 8 (hereafter GAO, *Hazardous Wastes*); John M. Broder, "U.S. Military Leaves Toxic Trail Overseas," *Los Angeles Times,* June 18, 1990.
4. GAO, *Hazardous Wastes,* 33. The unclassified version of the study released by the GAO deleted the names of the bases and the countries where they were located.

5. Michael Renner, "Assessing the Military's War on the Environment," in *State of the World, 1991,* ed. Lester R. Brown et al. (New York: W. W. Norton, 1991), 133, 135; Stephen Dycus, *National Defense and the Environment* (Hanover, N.H.: University Press of New England, 1996), 54, 80.

6. Adm. Eugene Carroll, "U.S. Military Bases and the Environment: A Time for Responsibility," address to the First International Conference on U.S. Military Toxins and Bases Clean-up, Manila, November 23–26, 1997, http://www.yonip.com/main/articles/responsibility.html, accessed October 11, 2007. See also Richard A. Wegman and Harold G. Bailey Jr., "The Challenge of Cleaning Up Military Waste When U.S. Bases Are Closed," *Ecology Law Quarterly* 21 (1994): 937–38; Benjamin Pimental, "Deadly Legacy, Dangerous Ground: Left over Bombs, Chemicals Wreak Havoc at Former U.S. Bases in Philippines," *San Francisco Chronicle,* July 5, 2001.

7. John Lindsay-Poland, *Emperors in the Jungle: The Hidden History of the U.S. in Panama* (Durham, N.C.: Duke University Press, 2003), 51–55, 61–73.

8. Ibid., 61, 139.

9. Renner, "Assessing the Military's War on the Environment," 134; Dycus, *National Defense and the Environment,* 5, 80; Seth Shulman, *The Threat at Home: Confronting the Toxic Legacy of the U.S. Military* (Boston: Beacon Press, 1992).

10. David S. Painter, "Oil," in *Encyclopedia of American Foreign Policy: Studies of the Principal Movements and Ideas,* 2nd ed., ed. Alexander DeConde, Richard Dean Burns, and Fredrik Logevall, 3 vols. (New York: Charles Scribners' Sons, 2002), 3:1–20.

11. Robert Goralski and Russell W. Freeburg, *Oil and War: How the Deadly Struggle for Fuel in WW II Meant Victory or Defeat* (New York: William Morrow, 1987), 167.

12. U.S. Department of Defense, Office of the Under Secretary of Defense for Acquisition, Technology, and Logistics, *More Capable Warfighting through Reduced Fuel Burden: Report of the Defense Science Board Task Force on Improving Fuel Efficiency of Weapons Platforms,* http://www.acq.osd.mil/dsb/reports/fuel.pdf (2001), p. 13, accessed October 6, 2007.

13. Simon Duke, *United States Military Forces and Installations in Europe* (Oxford: Oxford University Press, 1989), 352–56.

14. Shulman, *Threat at Home,* 110.

15. Quoted in Sandars, *America's Overseas Garrisons,* 151.

16. U.S. Department of Defense, *More Capable Warfighting through Reduced Fuel Burden ... ,* p. 3, accessed October 11, 2007.

17. Vaclav Smil, *Energy at the Crossroads: Global Perspectives and Uncertainties* (Cam-bridge, Mass.: MIT Press, 2003), 81.

18. U.S. Department of Defense, Defense Energy Support Center, *Energy Support for Global Missions: Fact Book FY 2003,* 56.

19. Renner, "Assessing the Military's War on the Environment," 137–40. The U.S. military also used large amounts of ozone-depleting substances such as halons and chlorofluorocarbons.

20. Ann Markusen, Peter Hall, Scott Campbell, and Sabina Deitrick, *The Rise of the Gun-belt: The Military Revamping of Industrial America* (New York: Oxford University Press, 1991).

21. Steven A. Schneider, *The Oil Price Revolution* (Baltimore: Johns Hopkins University Press, 1983), 60.

22. Arjun Makhijani, Stephen I. Schwartz, and William J. Weida, "Nuclear Waste Management and Environmental Remediation," in *Atomic Audit: The Costs and Consequences of U.S. Nuclear*

Weapons since 1940, ed. Stephen I. Schwartz (Washington, D.C.: Brookings Institution Press, 1998), 353–93; J. R. McNeill, *Something New under the Sun: An Environmental History of the Twentieth-Century World* (New York: W. W. Norton, 2000), 342–43; Claus Bernes, *Will Time Heal Every Wound? The Environmental Legacy of Human Activities* (Stockholm: Swedish Environmental Protection Agency, 2001), 147; Len Ackland, *Making a Real Killing: Rocky Flats and the Nuclear West* (Albuquerque: University of New Mexico Press, 2002); U.S. Department of Defense, "Departmental Issues Annual Environmental Cleanup Report for Fiscal 2001," press release, April 11, 2002.

23. M. S. El-Shobosky and Y. G. Al-Saedi, "The Impact of the Gulf War on the Arabian Environment," *Atmospheric Environment* 27A (1993): 95–108.

24. Rodolphe de Koninck, *Deforestation in Viet Nam* (Ottawa: International Development Research Centre, 1999), 12.

25. Arthur P. Westing, *Warfare in a Fragile World: Military Impact on the Human Environment* (London: Taylor and Francis, 1980); Arthur P. Westing, *Environmental Hazards of War* (Newbury Park, CA: Sage Publishers, 1990).

26. Bertrand Charrier, "Human and Ecological Consequences of the Gulf War's Environmental Damages in Kuwait," www.gci.ch/GreenCrossPrograms/legacy/UNCCKUWAIT.html (Geneva: UN Compensation Commission, 2000).

27. *EcoCompass,* "The Environmental Impacts of War," www.islandpress.org/eco-compass/war/war.html (2002); Samira A. S. Omar, E. Briskey, R. Misak, and A. A. S. O. Asem, "The Gulf War Impact on Terrestrial Environment of Kuwait: An Overview," paper presented to the First International Conference on Addressing Environmental Consequences of War, organized by the Environmental Law Institute and held at the Smithsonian Institution, Washington, DC, in 1998.

28. Robert Fisk, cited in *EcoCompass,* "The Environmental Impacts of War."

Questions for Reflection

In these Perspectives excerpts, the authors explore the environmental consequences of the world wars. As you reflect on how our mortal conflicts affect our climate, then and now, answer the following questions.

1. Take a minute and consider the weather conditions in WWI. In what ways did weather become part of the experience of war?

2. What battle (and when) bears the dubious distinction of being the first to deploy chemical weapons? What exactly was used? Describe its impact on men and local plants and animals (note the testimony of the British doctor here).

3. The author uses the German term *Schicksalsgemeinschaft* to describe the environmental impact of WWI. What is meant by this term? What to you is most important about this idea?

4. Describe the shift in thinking about national security after WWII and the related military buildup (including military bases).

5. According to the authors, the military buildup affected the surrounding ecosystems. How so? Note a couple of examples.

6. According to this excerpt, what overseas military base caused the most environmental damage? Describe the impact.

7. "The environmental damage caused by the U.S. military was greater at home than abroad." What evidence is used to support this assertion? Note the idea of causation.

8. Understanding causation is one of the most complex tasks of the historian, and rarely does a single cause explain everything about a major historical event. In the instances noted above, can you think of other explanations that may account for changes to the environment?

Activities Menu

Your instructor may assign one or more of the following learning activities:

Prewriting Exercise

Take a minute and write a paragraph (half page of notebook paper) on what you know about how WWI affected the landscape of Europe.

Media

Select a relevant video program from one of the following and write a one-page (double-spaced) reaction.

- TED Talk
- Munk Debates
- C-SPAN
- Crash Course

Source Search

Select and read two related primary sources found online at the Modern History Sourcebook and incorporate them into your discussion.

Class Discussion I

Use the questions above as the basis of a class discussion. Write out your answers ahead of time so that you can participate intelligently.

Class Discussion II

Use the questions above to talk about the parallels between the environmental impact of the world wars and those since 9/11. Are there similarities? If so, what are they? What differences are there?

Role-Playing Exercise

Divide the class into national security and environmental security "teams." Have a couple of students represent each side's perspective on which type of security best secures our future.

Suggested Reading

Dorothee Brantz, "Environments of Death: Trench Warfare on the Western Front, 1914–1918," in *War and the Environment: Military Destruction in the Modern Age* (2009)

J.R. McNeill and David Painter, "The Global Environment Footprint of the U.S. Military, 1978–2003)," in *War and the Environment: Military Destruction in the Modern Age* (2009)

Marilyn Shevin-Coetzee and Frans Coetzee, *World War I: A History in Documents* (2010)

Marilyn Shevin-Coetzee and Frans Coetzee, *The World in Flames: A WWII Sourcebook* (2010)

Sean McMeekin, *The Russian Origins of the First World War* (2011)

Chapter 6

Chapter Skill	Interpreting Sources
Chapter Issue	Individuals & History
Chapter Objectives (Students will...)	• Identify three specific ways in which individuals can be caught up in major historical developments • Assess three current perspectives on individuals and history • Demonstrate in a short essay on individuals and history the ability to interpret historical sources
Assignments and Assessments	1. Read the Setup Narrative 2. Listen to the Lecture(s) 3. Read the Perspectives excerpts 4. Compose a three-page Essay in answer to the assigned prompt 5. Take a brief "check-up" Quiz

Setup Narrative: Individuals & History

Ordinary individuals can sometimes have a brush with history. A common, humdrum existence can suddenly be transformed into a dramatic story of rescue or survival as people are caught up in events that change the course of history. The historical record—and the people who fill it—are never the same. Sometimes those experiences make heroes of unlikely characters. Others are implicated in horrendous crimes that shadow them and their families for generations.

World War I set in motion a radical realignment of cultural and political forces that forced individuals to make extremely thorny choices. It came first in the country most devastated by war—Russia. There the hungry, radicalized urban population of Petrograd refused to submit to the last tsar and, in the chaos that followed, found themselves subjects of another realm: that of the world's first socialist state. The most doctrinaire and intrigue-consumed of the Russian Marxists, Vladimir Lenin's Bolsheviks set about remaking the largest, most northern country on the planet into a workers' state, a communist society. All the edifices of the old regime had to come down. The monarchy, the powerful commercial and political elites, the Russian Orthodox Church, all had to be fought with the same fervor as the recent world war—and for better reasons, it was argued, reasons that justified the spread of the revolution across the leading cultures of the West: Germany, Italy, France, and Britain.

Radical realignments did occur in those places, but for different reasons and on a different footing. Workers did not create their own states in Great Britain and France, though they were supported by labor-oriented governments. Italy and Germany were another story. Wartime devastation created the perfect conditions for the rise of virulently nationalistic regimes whose mission was to captivate the will of the masses. Dictators were helped into power by populations desperate for economic recovery and national pride, and by 1930 right-wing, fascist regimes had come to power by the ballot box rather than the barricade. Their domestic policies, if we can so dignify them, were enmeshed with territorial expansion, first in Europe, then beyond. They made war on their own people before turning their attention to enemies abroad. Hitler and Mussolini took authority to rule by decree, created a leader cult, controlled their armies with party paramilitary troops, neutralized political opposition with a beefed-up (and beefy) police force, censored the press, centralized the economy, and brazenly undertook aggressive foreign policies in the face of the restrictions of the Treaty of Versailles. Hitler in particular, after assuming emergency powers, closing Germany's upper house of parliament (the *Reichsrat*) and labor unions, and purging opposition within the Nazi ranks, set about making war on Germany's Jews. Several discriminatory laws were already on the books by 1935, but in that year, the Nuremberg Laws stripped Jews of German citizenship, prohibited marriage between Jews and "Germans," and defined a Jew as anyone with at least one Jewish grandparent (which happened to include members of the Nazi brass, Hitler himself among them). For his part, Josef Stalin forced farmers into collectives and workers into industrial combines, created an internal passport system to better surveil, and purged the party and military of suspected enemies to the tune of 70% of the party and some 35,000 army officers—on the eve of the titanic clash with the German *Wehrmacht*. And if all that wasn't enough, the shocked populations of these powers then entered WWII, the most dramatic, lethal war in history.

How were individuals to understand their place in all of this? How were they to see themselves in what seemed a cosmic, future-building drama? Were they simply cogs in the wheel, another brick in the wall, or were they something more? It took people into the depths of their nation's history, and of major issues in religion and philosophy as well. And for good reason, the meaning of their individuality was at stake. One of the few silver linings of WWII is the vast and precious record of personal accounts that have survived and that speak to these very questions. Carefully read a sampling of those accounts below as you think about individuals and history.

Lecture
Pay attention to the chapter lecture(s), either online or in class.

Tips on Interpreting Sources

+ There's nothing like listening to an eyewitness to history, but be careful. That's only one view of events. Be sure to interpret sources, especially first-hand accounts, with bias in mind. Bias in the study of the past does not necessarily mean "skewed." It means having a point of view or perspective. That's all of us.

+ Don't assume that your source is representative of the times. It's still important even if it isn't, but be sure to look at multiple sources to get multiple perspectives (like those in this chapter).

+ Last but not least, make sure your sources are legitimate. Nations and empires have been constructed on houses of cards called forgeries. Over time people have gotten very good at this.

Jungvolk and Hitler Youth

by Frederic C. Tubach

The great attention paid to the young reveals a central aspect of Nazi ideology, that of a utopia based on ethnic solidarity.[1] A new Germany would be built by brushing away the old, weak, and decrepit, in short, all those who no longer had the drive necessary to radically transform society. In embracing the young generation, the regime also challenged most traditional vehicles of inculcation, including the churches as moral guides, the schools and their cultural norms, and even the family, with its stabilizing, moderating effect on an individual's behavior.

Some of us remember this frontal attack on traditional values much more than the anti-Semitic propaganda to which we were exposed. It hit closer to home because it undermined authority as we knew it. The Nazis replaced traditions with a new legitimacy that granted the "freedom" (in actuality, the license) to give one's instincts free rein, as long as they were released in the name of the Nazi cause. Of course, this was the Nazis' intention: to redefine the superego in their terms, then to wed the new superego to the instincts and to eliminate the self as the battleground of desires and restraints. For example, many of my generation came from Christian homes and associated prayer with the beginning of the evening meal. In *Jungvolk* and Hitler Youth camps, before meals were served we were encouraged to raise a ruckus with our cutlery while screaming as loudly as possible, "We are hungry, hungry, hungry, give us some grub or else!" This replaced the saying of grace, perverting prayer to Nazi ends. The net result of this mix of superego with the instincts was, of course, the destruction of moral sensibilities and civilized behavior.

I experienced a similar incident, which I described in *An Uncommon Friendship: From Opposite Sides of the Holocaust*:

> During the *Bannausleselager* [preparatory camp], one of the twelve boys in my dormitory had brought along a condom. We blew it up like a balloon and floated it out of the window into the courtyard. Camp leaders seemed enraged by this prank.

Their investigation traced the infraction to our quarters, and we were grilled for hours, pressured to reveal the culprit, and threatened with severe punishments. At the same time, however, I detected a certain ambiguity in these interrogations, which obviously implied an underlying compliment: "Ihr seid Kerle" (You're real men). We stuck together, refused to betray the instigator, and escaped punishment. The double message of our superiors linked a number of factors—sexuality, transgression, regulations, and male solidarity—that served both to maintain order and to inculcate in us a sense of rebellion and team spirit. They wanted to make us capable of doing anything in service of the grand Nazi design. They encouraged us to develop into a controlled horde, a gang, really, legitimized and led by the greatest tribal chief of all time, who sat in Berlin.[2]

Hitler had provided a blueprint for this dangerous mix of instincts and superego already in *Mein Kampf* (first published in 1925). He later wrote in *An seine Jugend* (To his youth, 1937), "It is unbelievable that it is prophesied that many a young person will end up on the gallows for personal characteristics that would be of priceless value if they became the common heritage of the entire *Volk*."[3] Hitler's early plans to integrate the asocial impulses of the young to serve his system were later elaborated on in leadership handbooks written for those in charge of training the young: "With their friends they [the young] form adventurous hordes, which at times develop a frightening fantasy for dangerous undertakings and 'uncivilized' ideas. A strange world of values, tightly knit and closed, appears before our eyes, quite independent of the views of the parental home or the school. The protection of the home and bourgeois behavior are despised. Industriousness in school is discarded for the sake of courage and physical prowess."[4]

Abstract as this may sound now, at the time conflicts between the younger generation and their elders brought tears, uncertainty in terms of roles, confusing disruptions in family life, and divided loyalties. In other words, these battles were very real for my generation. Occasionally teenagers turned against their parents, but most of these struggles were carried out behind closed doors, some of the more dramatic fights taking place between parents skeptical of the Nazi movement and their sons and daughters who were enthusiastic members of the *Jungvolk*, *Jungmädel*, *Bund Deutscher Mädel*, or *Hitlerjugend*. Such divided loyalties occurred in almost all spheres of private life.

• • •

The organized activities of the *Jungvolk* (boys ages ten to fourteen) and the Hitler Youth (fourteen- to eighteen-year-old boys) were inextricably linked to sports. While membership was not mandatory between 1933 and 1935, by the middle of the decade membership had become compulsory. All of the members of my generation of both sexes that I interviewed had belonged. The attractions of these Nazi organizations for the young were found in the "big show" and in "games," catchwords that describe constellations of events and programs. Violence played virtually no role. Several German Jews my age told me after the war that early on they had wanted to join the *Hitlerjugend*, with all its attractive singing, marching, and athletic activities. They begged their parents to let them, only to be told that Jews were not allowed.

While the Nazi party provided the general ideology for the youth organizations, no clearly defined national agenda guided weekly meetings. Consequently, these meetings varied greatly, depending on local leaders' fanaticism or personal preferences. Occasionally, higher-ups in the movement would visit and lecture on the virtues of being part of a new Germany. By singing or reading heroic tales of the Germanic past while gathered around campfires, the Hitler Youth often adopted traditions of pre-Nazi youth movements.

Probably the most popular of the Hitler Youth activities—for boys, anyway—were the maneuvers in the countryside, or *Geländespiele* (they were not called "war games," even though that's what they were). The aim was to conquer a particular point in the landscape—a tower, village main square, bridge, or similar object. Each participant had a band tied around his arm, either red or blue. Once an opponent had caught you and torn off your band, you were "dead" and could no longer participate. One of the exciting aspects of the *Geländespiele* was that the normal geography within which one lived was transformed for a day into territory to be defended or attacked by the young, beyond the control of our elders.

In preparation for these games, we were taught to focus on what we heard and saw, and we learned how to describe our physical surroundings so as to help our superiors plan an attack or defense. Strategy sessions were coupled with discussions of tactics. In this way the childhood game of hide-and-seek was translated into quasi-military activities. Variations abounded, as in this description from a 1934 book: "A boy hides in the forest and utters a few loud shrieks. The other boys look for the screamer, but they have to move cautiously because anyone struck by the beam of his flashlight is considered eliminated. The goal is to catch the boy who had screamed."[5] This was difficult, and it could only be done if certain boys sacrificed themselves in a frontal attack, while one sneaked up from behind to catch the screamer. The victory went to the team as a whole, however, and never to an individual—early training in "group-think" or, more accurately, in the value of sacrificing oneself for the common good. Occasionally, these games became violent, as when one village was pitted against another and old animosities characteristic of rural life broke out.

An important aspect of the Hitler Youth and *Jungvolk* was their hierarchical structure. As one ascended in rank, one gained control over an ever-increasing number of youngsters in the quasi-military exercises and marches. Leadership talents were recognized and promoted at an accelerated pace. Prowess in sports was particularly rewarded.

Next to weekly meetings, the authorities showed films created specifically for the young. None was more effective than *Hitlerjunge Quex,* depicting the life of a teenager who wants to join the Hitler Youth but whose father has signed him up for the *Jugendinternationale* of the Communist Party.[6] A deep political split in his family drove Quex's mother to suicide. Deeply moved by his mother's death, the young Quex becomes an activist for the Nazi cause and is murdered by the Communists as a traitor. The movie focuses on the natural preoccupations of young Germans: family conflicts, tragic consequences, divided political loyalties, and the need for personal guidance. Most of us saw the film. For many of my generation it became the defining moment of their anticommunism in the thirties. Later on, Soviet communism came to embody the evil that many of us had seen in *Hitlerjunge Quex.*

But the meetings and indoctrination, of course, did not constitute everyday life in all its variety. The youth organizations of the Hitler era (with the exception of the *Ordensburgen,* special schools for training the future Nazi elite) cannot be compared to present-day Islamic fundamentalist *madrassas,* in which youths live at the schools and are immersed in extremist religious propaganda twenty-four hours a day. In Nazi Germany, members of the Hitler Youth and *Jungvolk* had functioning family lives and commitments and loyalties outside of the youth meetings, in communities that operated on many levels and according to old habits.

• • •

The Nazis did not have a large contingent of trained ideologues to shape the canons of German history to their ends. The fact that Nazi concepts were so vague and unsupported by historical facts gave license to the fanatics to say whatever moved them, as long as it stimulated hatred and prejudice.

Occasionally, one of the higher-up Hitler Youth leaders from the district office would appear at one of our weekly meetings in Kleinheubach. All *Hitlerjugend* and *Jungvolk* members had to assemble on the soccer field to listen to his strident speech, in which he became increasingly animated. One day, he claimed, when the Nazi utopia had arrived, we would all throw away our watches (as a sign of a decadent civilization) and allow ourselves to be guided by the sun, moon, and stars. This surely did not reflect any official Nazi doctrine; rather, it was a spontaneous, creative (not to mention ludicrous) idea of his own making. None of the boys in attendance discussed this prospect afterward, because most of us would have loved to receive a wristwatch for Christmas, if only our parents had been able to afford it. In fact, most of us sensed the distance between such hyperbolic propaganda and our natural, youthful resistance to authority, Nazi or otherwise.

The Nazi call for an "ideal youth" (that is, ideally suited to their ends), of course, never fit the young generation as a whole, and Hitler decided early on, very much in keeping with his revolution from above, to select from the young German population those he considered good prospects for membership in his future elite. "My pedagogy is hard," he wrote. "Whatever is weak must be hammered away. In my *Ordensburgen* ... a youth will grow up that will horrify the world. I want to have a violent, lordly, fearless, cruel youth. They must be full of youthful vitality. They have to suffer and conquer pain. Nothing gentle and weak in them must be left. The free, magnificent wild animal must flash forth in their eyes."[7]

The wilderness played a part in the dreams of German youth, but not as part of the military groups they were supposed to join or organize. Rather, the American Wild West with its Indians, as evoked in the novels of Karl May, was loved by young Germans. May's numerous stories came in conflict, however, with the stories that Nazis deemed ideal for young Germans. So the leadership developed a counterstrategy of emphasizing Germanic heroes; as one Nazi authority pointed out, "Winnetou and Old Shatterhand were the heroes of our youth, so all we had was the courage and bravery of a foreign people. But what are all the requisites of Indian life worth now—the peace pipe and feathered headdress—compared to the Germanic sword, the ornaments and tools of our Germanic ancestors, as we make them accessible to our youth? The courage of Siegfried, the loyalty of Hagen, and the love of Kriemhilde tell us more than the most beautiful stories of other peoples."[8]

Despite such Nazi efforts, their pedagogy couldn't compete effectively with the fantasies that Karl May evoked. After all, the Germanic epics were part of the canon taught in school and thus were associated with study and exams, not attractive flights of fancy to a distant, foreign land. Nazi pedagogy was instead more persuasive when it attacked modern art and abstract painting as another decadent symptom of "Weimar chaos." The widely discussed 1937 Nazi Degenerate Art exhibition convinced most Germans that expressionist paintings were a sign of moral decay. What Nazis wanted in art was the redundant reproduction of their reality.

In the indoctrination meetings of the Hitler Youth, and to some degree in geography and history classes taught by teachers who believed in the Nazi cause, much was made of the concept of *Lebensraum*. At first, this "living space" necessary for the German people to thrive was defined as lands cultivated by Germanic tribes, within which "the cultural treasures and the racial quality of the Nordic peoples were able to flourish throughout Europe."[9] A traditional linguistic sleight of hand—defining Indo-European as Indo-Germanic—allowed the Nazis to use their racist, expansionist notions to include lands to the east. As the Allies closed in on Germany, the definition of *Lebensraum* was increasingly redefined as the battlefield for the survival of the "Germanic race."

My generation listened to that propaganda and had difficulty believing the survival of the *race* was threatened. Nor was survival of the Nazi Party on our minds. But we *were* concerned with the survival of our fatherland, of Germany as our nation. Our elders had passed down to us the idea that World War I had been a war between nations, not between races. But after the fatal handshake between Hindenburg and Hitler that legitimized the Nazi movement in the eyes of cultural traditionalists, patriotism became conflated and therefore confused with Nazism. While Nazi teachers often attempted to weave propaganda into classroom lessons, such efforts were not necessarily effective. One interviewee told me that a common strategy used in his school to avoid a feared examination was to ask a fanatic teacher a question about the Nazi movement. In his enthusiasm to respond, the teacher would forget to administer the exam, instead praising the students for their astute political interests.

Whatever effect the Hitler Youth had in shaping the minds of young Germans, I believe it was not as great as one might think by watching all the *Jungvolk* and Hitler Youth marchers, fifers, and drummers in films about the Third Reich—and despite the fact that youth naturally enjoyed these activities immensely. The leaders of these organizations were, of course, convinced Nazis, but they came from the same social and familial environments as the rest of us, where their rank mattered less than the social status of their family. Hitler Youth leaders sat next to us in our classes, they sweated through the exams with the rest of us, and we were all aware of their fathers' professions. In short, the Nazi simplifications and slogans could not destroy the diversity of educational experiences the young received during the twelve years of the Third Reich. It mattered a great deal, for example, whether you attended a *Gymnasium* that emphasized classical languages (Greek or Latin) or a *Realgymnasium* that stressed modern languages and the sciences.

To be sure, the Nazis disseminated educational guidelines throughout Germany, but they were full of vague concepts that lacked any cultural canon to support them. Terms such as "the sphere of the people's soul" or "the biology of the innermost essence and laws that determine the fate of a *Volk*" were of no use in schools accustomed to a defined curriculum.[10] The Nazis were never able to develop an official curriculum to supplant the highly structured, traditional curricula of German *Gymnasien,* and pro-Nazi teachers usually stuck to their subjects, though they might try to give them an ideological twist.

The Nazis did develop a kind of variant school system in the form of the *Ordensburgen,* which were dedicated to training and indoctrinating a future Nazi elite. But these schools were reserved for a very small percentage of the student population. Forty or so students might be selected from a *Gymnasium* class and sent to a *Bannausleselager* (preparatory camp), from which four or five boys with the greatest potential for becoming devout Nazis were promoted to an *Ordensburg.*

Limits in the Nazis' control of German society became evident when they stepped outside their organizational framework. For instance, they offered a Nazi wedding ritual as an alternative to the traditional Christian wedding ceremonies, but these new ceremonies never gained much popularity. Nevertheless, anyone who married during the years of Hitler's regime, whether in a traditional religious ceremony or its Nazi variant, received a copy of *Mein Kampf* with the *Führer*'s best wishes and printed signature. People generally shelved this book unread.

In 1938, the year before World War II was proclaimed, the Nazis declared *ein Jahr der Verständigung* (year of communication/understanding); they also made an effort to contact youth movements in other countries and bring them to one of their big shows—a tactic that had served them well just two years before when they invited the world to the Olympic Games. The Nazis believed that if young people from abroad were to experience one of their Hitler Youth meetings, they would, as historian Michael Buddrus puts it, "be freed from the belief that hatred of other nations and thoughts of revenge were being propagated in Germany."[11]

The sense of a dawning utopia in Germany faded in November of that same year with the Night of the Broken Glass *(Reichspogromnacht* or *Kristallnacht).* Ten months later, with the beginning of the war on September 1, 1939, it disappeared altogether. War spelled the end of false dreams. Hitler's earlier slogans about youth being the nation's hope and future and young people acting as the subjects of their own fate changed radically. We now realized that what he really intended was for our generation to be "hart wie Kruppstahl, zäh wie Leder, flink wie Windhunde" (hard as the steel of Krupp, tough as leather, and swift as greyhounds)—notions first propagated in Riefenstahl's *Triumph of the Will.* Most of us felt uncertain whether we could rise to this challenge. *Tough as leather* might be all right for some, *swift as greyhounds* for others, but to ask all three utopian virtues of most young Germans was too much. Hitler remained uncompromising when he proclaimed his educational goals in a speech of 1938:

> This younger generation will learn nothing less than to think and act German. And when this boy and this girl enter our organization at the age of ten and for the first time breathe the fresh air and begin to feel things, they will then be moved from the *Jungvolk* to the Hitler Youth, and there we will keep them for another four years, and after that we will most definitely not return them back into the hands of those who have created social classes and prestige, but we will take them immediately into the party, or the Worker's Division of the party, or into the SA or SS and so on. And if by then they have not yet become complete National Socialists, we will

assign them to workers' brigades, and there they will be subjected to severe training for six or seven months. And if then there is anything left in them about social class or personal privilege, the army will take them over for further treatment. And they will never be free again, for their entire life.[12]

His ultimate goal was to turn an entire generation into robots, or as Dr. Robert Ley, one of his lieutenants, put it succinctly, "The pulse of the blood must blend in with the rhythm of the machine."[13]

• • •

It is my belief that the majority of German youths neither could nor wanted to live up to the most extreme, utopian fantasies of the Nazis. School, church, and family continued to form a powerful counterbalance, and most of our teachers, priests, and parents had a different educational agenda. The Nazis themselves must have been aware of the limits of their propagandistic reach. In an opinion poll in 1937 that queried female members of a Nazi labor organization, political education ranked tenth on their scale of interests, well behind a preference for singing (which ranked first), sports and dancing, hiking and trips, festivals and celebrations, and basic job training.[14] Not only this poll, but my childhood memories, my interviews of older Germans, and archival material support my belief that in the everyday life of the German people, personal interests and preferences were more important to most individuals than the political hyperventilation of the Nazis as they attempted to shape the public sphere. Catholic children continued to take communion and their Protestant compatriots continued to be confirmed; fathers went to work, women scrubbed floors and cared for children, and young people attended school. All of this continued during the Nazi years, even though it did not make it into the history books.

Yet ultimately, the traditional influences of families, schools, and churches failed to stop the war machine from revving up to its full, catastrophic force. Whatever remained of individualism and dissenting opinions lost all public relevance after Hitler attacked the Soviet Union. Young men were ordered to fight in the war, and off they went. As draftees, they had no choice. Many were convinced they were fighting a patriotic battle for Germany's survival. Tragically, a sufficient minority performed the Nazis' bidding, escalating battles into a total war and unleashing the genocide.

Notes

1. After 1935, all German youths, both boys and girls, belonged to the Nazi youth organizations, by law, with the exception of the usual groups: Jews, Gypsies (Roma), and the mentally and physically handicapped.
2. Bernat Rosner and Frederic C. Tubach, with Sally Patterson Tubach, *An Uncommon Friendship: From Opposite Sides of the Holocaust* (Berkeley: University of California Press, 2001), 103.
3. Adolf Hitler, *Adolf Hitler an seine Jugend* (Berlin and Munich: Zentralverlag der NSDAP, 1937), 2.
4. Albrecht Günther, *Geist der Jungmannschaft* (Hamburg: Hanseatische Verlagsanstalt, 1934), 37.
5. E. Mischlich, *Führer im Geländesport für Hitlerjugend und Geländesportschulen,* ed. E. Hägele (Leipzig: Armanen Verlag, 1934), 55.
6. This movie can be viewed in its entirety at http://de.metapedia.org/wiki/Hitlerjunge_Quex; short segments can also be found on YouTube.

7. Adolf Hitler, in Walther Hofer, ed., *Der Nationalsozialismus. Dokumente 1933–1945* (Frankfurt: Fischer Bücherei, 1957), 88.
8. Gert Bennewitz, "Die geistige Wehrerziehung der deutschen Jugend," in *Schriften für Politik und Auslandskunde,* ed. F. A. Six (Berlin: Dünnhaupt Verlag, 1940), 16.
9. Fritz Brennecke, ed., *Vom deutschen Volk und seinem Lebensraum. Handbuch. Die Schulungsarbeit in der HJ [Hitlerjugend]* (Munich: Zentralverlag der NSDAP, 1937), 81.
10. Ernst Anrich, "Neue Schulgestaltung aus nationalsozialistischem Denken," in *Kulturpolitische Schriftenreihe,* Heft 4 (Stuttgart: W. Kohlhammer, 1933), 66-67.
11. Michael Buddrus, *Totale Erziehung für den totalen Krieg. Hitlerjugend und nationalsozialistische Jugend-politik* (Munich: K. G. Saur, 2003), 66.
12. Adolf Hitler, quoted in Bernhard Haupert, *Jugend zwischen Kreuz und Hakenkreuz. Biographische Rekonstruktion als Alltagsgeschichte des Faschismus* (Frankfurt: Suhrkamp, 1991), 12.
13. Dr. Robert Ley, *Deutschland ist schöner geworden,* ed. Hans Dauer and Walter Kiehl (Berlin: Mehden Verlag, 1936), 3.
14. Ulrich Hermann and Ulrich Nassen, eds., *Formative Ästhetik im Nationalsozialismus. Intentionen, Medien und Praxisformen totalitärer ästhetischer Herrschaft und Beherrschung* (Weinheim and Basel: Beltz Verlag, 1993), 157.

In Battle in Europe

by Emiel W. Owens

THROUGH THE RUHR POCKET

As we expanded from our bridgehead in the vicinity of Verden, the rapid retreat of the Germans slowed as their resistance grew. As the battle raged farther into the Ruhr Pocket, the defenders became more determined. Before leaving the bridgehead, an advance party was sent to survey the area around Dinslaken to find a place to set up an observation post. We also needed an adequate location for our guns in the vicinity of our selected targets to provide direct support for our advancing infantry attack forces. Because of the flexibility and accuracy of our guns, we were leaving this bridgehead almost in concert with our infantry. Things were fluid and moving fast. At 8:00 A.M. on March 24, our advance party of three soldiers and I left Verden and headed for Dinslaken, about twenty miles north. Since our infantry was clearing resistance pockets as we advanced, the trip took about two hours by jeep.

Upon entering the outskirts of Dinslaken, I saw a large two-story house with an apple orchard located on the corner of two intersecting streets. With the support of an infantry platoon, we worked our way over to the house. We could get a view of enemy defensive fortifications for miles, as well as a view of troop movements, which made the house ideal for an observation post. The orchard was suitable for the location of our guns. Upon approaching the house, I stopped while our advancing infantry units kept moving. As we neared the house, I noticed it had two double glass doors at the front entrance and a wooden door on the west side. By peeking through the front doors, I could see stairs leading to the second floor, so we decided to approach through the front entry. Extreme caution had to be exercised, as a house this size could be the headquarters for German army units or could be used as an enemy hideout. We had just thirty minutes remaining to secure our position, as the battalion with our column of guns was scheduled to arrive at 10:30 A.M.

I walked in first, followed by three soldiers in support position with their carbines drawn. After a quick search, I found the downstairs vacant. I quickly, but cautiously, started upstairs. I walked on the balls of my feet to maintain silence on the oak stairs. Halfway up the stairs I heard talking and saw a pair of shoes worn by someone at the top of the stairs. They looked like men's shoes, but then I remembered they also looked like the shoes I had observed the women wearing as they plowed in the fields.

I looked up and saw a middle-aged woman standing at the top of the stairs. Her hands were raised and she was hysterically yelling *"Nicht schiessen, nicht schiessen, bitte nicht schiessen"* (Don't shoot, don't shoot, please don't shoot). I knew she was from a working family by the clothes she wore. I responded to her in the broken German I knew. *"Nicht Schiessen, nicht Schiessen, Frau—nicht Schiessen"* (No shooting, no shooting, lady, no shooting). By this time, three other individuals appeared at the top of the stairs and stood beside her. I alerted my assistants to be prepared in case an armed soldier appeared so that he would not get a drop on us.

As we advanced to the top of the stairs, the four retreated a few steps backward into a small kitchen area. I discovered that they were eating breakfast when we entered their home: a boiled egg, a slice of brown bread, a piece of meat, and coffee being served family style. The middle-aged woman nervously took a boiled egg from the table and offered it to me. I thanked her but refused. She appeared to have calmed down somewhat and tried to smile. In addition to the middle-aged woman, the group consisted of a young woman in her midthirties, a teenage girl, and an older man. I kept a watchful eye on them while my assistants searched the upstairs for armed soldiers.

During the search I had one of my assistants, who spoke German, explain to them that we would need their home for a few days as a headquarters, after which they could return. They took turns putting a few clothes in a gray handbag and finished eating the breakfast they had left on the table. I am not sure if the old man lived there or was just having breakfast, as he made no preparation to leave. He just stood at the window, gazing out over a large meadow. Perhaps he had once been a soldier but was now too old, so he was just waiting for the war to end with the women and children.

When the middle-aged woman first saw me, the enemy, with my weapon drawn and standing halfway up her stairs, she was frightened and I could see the panic in her eyes. I think it was from seeing the enemy in her house; and in the Ruhr area of Germany, many had never seen an African American man other than in films, books, and newspapers. The younger woman seemed too calm. She never seemed excited or afraid, which made me suspicious. The young girl was a little frightened, but I think she was more concerned about whether or not we would harm them. I think at first she was not sure if I was an African man or an American. She may have seen the

American soldiers running while fighting in the streets, and they were all white, so I think she was confused. The old man seemed a little frightened, but mostly just apprehensive. I told them, through my interpreter, that they would have to leave and could live in a basement across the street for a few days. Then they could come back home. There was a big battle raging, and the basement would protect them. We were going to set our big guns up in their orchard, and we expected shelling from their soldiers. We had about ten minutes left before the arrival of our soldiers and guns, so I asked them to be out in five minutes and assured them we would do our best not to destroy their property.

Still, I remained vigilant while watching the young woman, suspicious that she might be a special agent. I had read in the *Stars and Stripes* about a soldier killed in the presence of a young German woman in Aachen. A few minutes before I walked out, the young woman asked me my name, *"Wie heissen Du?"* I was shocked and thought she was talking to someone else until I noticed she was looking at me. I told her, "Emiel Owens." The name got her attention, as she remembered Jessie Owens, plus Emil is a German name. She then walked up to me, rubbed her two fingers across my face and asked, *"Warum Du schwarz sind?"* (Why are you black?) *"Ist es die Sonne?"* (Is it the sun?) I told her the Negro race had many colors; it is not the sun, but race. She wanted a longer conversation, and so did I. I wanted to learn more about her. I had discovered that you cannot paint all Germans with one brush. I told her my time was up and for her to *"Gehen Sie schnell"* (leave quickly).

By this time, my guns were on the street, ready to be placed. We placed them among the fruit trees in her orchard, fired adjusting rounds, and were ready for our night firing. Our infantry was encountering stiff resistance in the center of the town and needed us. I saw the young woman again for the last time just before sunset that day, standing alone at the entrance of the cellar across the street from her home that we were occupying. The setting sun was in her face as she stood gazing toward our gun positions in her orchard. She had changed clothes to a pale blue outfit almost matching her steel blue eyes, but the relaxed composure she exhibited this morning seemed not to change.

This encounter stayed with me for a long time. As I first faced her, while going up the stairs that morning, I could see fear on her face but no panic. Foreign troops with black faces and drawn carbines occupying her home was a frightful experience for her, but she stayed calm as she became aware that we would not harm her. I later started thinking about my experience as a high school student with German American farmers at home. We were usually hired by them to pull corn during the peak corn-harvesting season. What I remembered most was that they ate four times a day, and someone would bring hot food to the field. They would lay a cloth on the ground, and everyone, including the hired hands, would sit to eat the food, which was served family style. This created a lasting impression, especially for youngsters who were struggling to get two meals daily at home.

We remained embroiled in battle for two days. Before we made our second advance in the Ruhr Pocket position, we were successfully occupied at Dinslaken. The position at Dinslaken was rather unusual for the size of our artillery because our battalion had the mission of covering a twelve-hundred-mil sector. All twelve of our guns were laid on a different centerline so that they could be massed on a five-hundred-mil sector in the center. Later, due to the risk of a counterattack by the Germans, all batteries were shifted to the left portion of the sector. At the close of the period, our battalion advanced to a position near Thurohdenwind with an azimuth of fire due east. During this cycle, 8,987 rounds were expended, the highest total for a month since we entered combat. This brought the total expended to date to 30,000 rounds. As we advanced farther into the interior of the Ruhr Pocket, we engaged in nearly three weeks of difficult and frustrating action. Although some cities surrendered at once, others made fanatical last stands in bombed-out streets and among the rubble in the middle of Germany's heartland.

Our advances became more frequent but for shorter distances. This gave us the opportunity to get a panoramic view of a once-proud nation that was now a conquered shell. During our advances, I observed untended fields pockmarked with foxholes and slit trenches covering the countryside. For the first time I saw that entire towns were devastated. The engine of my tractor roared hollowly through the streets of deserted villages, where not even the presence of migrating birds interrupted the lifelessness of the gutted buildings, the gaping shell holes, and the heaps of rubble. The silence in the towns was worse than the noise our shells made. Instinctively, we expected to hear the noises people make while going about their business. The silence, coupled with the sudden absence of the sounds of fighting, made a walk through any German town an eerie experience. The "sacred soils" of Germany had begun to feel the harsh hand of anger imposed by the wrath of would-be conquerors. The spectacle was not pleasant to behold.

War comes to Germany. *Source: European Stars and Stripes*, March 3, 1945, 1.

The scene is the same familiar confusion of war and peace. Our guns were located near a turn row on the edge of a wheat field on the outskirts of Buer. The soil was thawing in the warmer weather. These soggy fields made maneuvering large guns difficult because of the mud. Our commander's strategy with this advance was to deal with the German forces in the Ruhr Pocket by encircling the German units with two deep thrusts, as on the map on p. 97.

Our advance into Buer was part of a seven-army advance directly into German defenses. The drive started with massive artillery barrages on March 28, 1945. The Ninth Army had already reached the Rhine opposite Düsseldorf and continued north to join Canadian forces. Our Ninth Army had also captured the Rhine city of

The Ruhr Pocket under siege. *Source: European Stars and Stripes,* March 6, 1945, 1.

Muenchen-Gladbach, the home of Nazi propaganda minister Joseph Goebbels and one of the largest Nazi cities on the western front captured up to this point.

One day we found an old man walking aimlessly through our firing zone. We caught him by the arm and led him out to safety. I asked him about his town and if he knew Goebbels. He had gone to school with him and remembered the boy with the big round eyes and big mouth. There was a castle over to my right called Schloss Rheydt, which was the castle the Nazis had told the people of the city to give to the Goebbels out of gratitude. This town put up stiff resistance before it was captured, and the castle was never damaged.

After leaving Duisberg in total ruin from our air bombardment and fighting over the past three days, it was almost gratifying and a relief to enter the Rhine city of Krefeld. The city of about 120,000 had not been attacked by our bombers, so things were pretty well intact. Most of the stores in town were open. German women wearing overcoats were riding bicycles down the streets while carrying shopping bags. Businessmen were walking around with their brief-cases, although they were all old men. I noticed wide-eyed men and women standing on street corners, looking indirectly at us, seemingly surprised that they were not all being massacred. The hands of little children went up halfway in an attempt to wave before they caught them-selves and followed their elders' example of looking but not acknowledging our presence. I had never witnessed a scene like this before. The city was like an oasis, entirely intact with business going on as usual in the midst of ruins. When our forces had attacked on this morning, all the communications were intact, and food and water were in abundance. It took only one day for our forces to take the city.

As we approached the prime city of Düsseldorf, now in rubble, the sudden appearance of SS battle groups inside the city ready to mount fierce counterattacks caused anxious moments among our commanders. The end result was nearly three weeks of difficult and costly action in terms of lives lost. Although some towns and villages surrendered at once, the defenders of Düsseldorf made a fanatical last stand. Eighteen divisions and three weeks were required to end all resistance, but the scale of our victory astounded our commanders. By April 18, three German armies had been trapped and 317,000 German prisoners, including twenty-five generals, had been taken. When the all clear was given, I took a brief walk to get a clear picture in my mind of how a city could be totally destroyed under wartime conditions.

While walking, I saw an old man on the opposite side of the street. I crossed over to meet him. He appeared to be in a numb state, as if he had been hit by a shell, and was walking aimlessly. As I got near him, I asked him if the city would ever be built up again or whether a new site would be selected. He said, in fairly good English, that it would be rebuilt. As though to prove his point, he pointed to some women already cleaning bricks on the bombed-out buildings.

I returned to my gun position after about ten minutes of walking and immediately received a fire mission. In concert with the XVI Corps, we fired all night in troop support to silence incoming artillery barrages. It was about 4:30 A.M. when I received a cease-fire. My crew were exhausted, but we were fortunate in that there were no wounded. Tired and hungry, we all went to a makeshift mess hall. I was about half finished eating when I had the urge to go back and take a good look at one of the trails of my guns, which seemed to be shifting in the soft mud as a result of the constant firing all night. If this were the case, the guns would not fire true, as the trail would shift off center. After examining the trail for fifteen minutes, I began to make my way back to the mess hall.

As I was walking along, something hit right at my feet, and the splash literally covered me from head to toe with mud. I looked around to see what had happened and discovered that a German 88-mm artillery shell had landed almost between my legs. Fortunately, it did not detonate and explode. Instead, the fuse of the shell landed in the soft ground on a flat trajectory and, as a result, did not have the force required to detonate. That soft wet soil, which moments before I had wanted to curse for throwing off my gun trail, had actually saved my life. If the shell had hit the ground at just a slight angle, it would have exploded. A section chief, who had been having breakfast, was watching from the mess hall and saw what happened. He came rushing over and gave me a piece of cloth to clean my face, as the mud had temporarily blinded me. I think I was involuntarily shaking. I was led to our medic clinic, and two hours later I was put on a jeep bound for a rest and rehabilitation camp in Belgium. The army sent soldiers who had undergone extended combat stress there for rehabilitation, usually for a week or more. This incident added to the other occasions in recent months that I had cheated death. Four hours after I left the field, I was sitting in the office of an army psychiatrist in Belgium.

The next page shows a photo taken after my first psychiatric session in the rehabilitation clinic. The date was April 24, 1945. For all practical purposes, the war was over for me. The doctor demanded that I remain in a quiet, restful environment for at least seven days. On April 25 our corps split up. Some elements fanned out in the Ruhr Pocket to eliminate resistance pockets, while the others continued on to the Elbe River. These elements did not cross the river because of the advancing resistance forces from the east. While our forces cleared up the remaining resistance in the western part of Germany, the Russians attacked Berlin in a fierce battle. Inside the city, Adolf Hitler and a few of his followers were sheltered in a bunker deep beneath the Reich chancellery. Berlin was turned to rubble as German units resisted to the very end.

When the city surrendered on May 2, three hundred thousand Russians and an unknown number of Germans lay dead among the ruins. Two days before the fall of Berlin, Hitler committed suicide. Despite the fact that he was dead, German soldiers still fought fanatically until the end. Many German units fought their way to the west to surrender to American or British units so as not to fall into the hands of the Russians.

On May 4, 1945, German forces in northern Europe surrendered unconditionally to Field Marshal Montgomery. Three days later, the remaining forces in the west surrendered to General Eisenhower's staff. On May 7, General Eisenhower announced that the mission of the Allied forces in Europe was complete. May 8, however, was designated as V-E (Victory in Europe) Day. In some remote areas, fighting continued until May 11.

Nazi Germany had been destroyed. After six long, bitter years, the war in Europe was over. Members of our army picked up copies of the *Stars and Stripes* proclaiming V-E Day as they came off the press.

During my stay at a rehabilitation camp in Brussels, Belgium, May 1945.

The task of the ground soldier who carried the war to the enemy had been successfully completed. Supreme Commander Gen. Dwight D. Eisenhower's determined stewardship of a complex and, at intervals, contentious coalition force made the successful conclusion of a difficult campaign possible. We, as indomitable ground soldiers, transformed the possibilities of high-level decision making into victory on the ground. This, in spite of incredible harsh weather, difficult terrain, and an astute and determined foe. From my point of view, our infantry had the most difficult role to carry. General Eisenhower once wrote that it was his infantry who had demonstrated the real heroism, which is the uncomplaining acceptance of unendurable conditions. But for their part, captured German soldiers often claimed to be most impressed not by American armor or infantry but by our artillery. They frequently remarked on our accuracy, the swiftness with which we acquired targets, and especially the prodigality with which artillery ammunition was expended. The fact that the liberal use of artillery saved countless American infantrymen seemed to escape many Germans, perhaps because it cost so many German lives. Despite my ability to recount its events, my journey through this war still remains for the most part truly beyond description.

THE WAR ENDS—SECURITY DUTIES

When the public announcement was made that Germany had been defeated and had unconditionally surrendered, the Belgian people poured into the streets dancing for joy. I first experienced that strange scene of the confusion of war and peace as the jeep returning me from my rest stop in Belgium entered Germany. As we drove along, I kept watching brigades of women in the hollow streets clearing rubbish from bombed-out buildings and craters half filled with water. There were more women brigades out on the streets than usual. The women had plow shafts in their hands and were walking behind the white oxen in an attempt to turn the half-frozen soil. They never looked up as we passed; they just kept slogging along. The black-and-white dairy cows that ran in terror when I last saw them a few weeks earlier kept walking among the trenches and half-frozen pastures in search of grass. As I rode along, I kept thinking how quiet and eerie it was, even with people going about their daily business.

Yes, it indeed was all quiet here on the western front. I recalled the time when I had left Germany about six nights earlier. I thought that hell itself had invaded and Satan had taken over our planet. Then the war was over and I had survived. I was saddened when I thought of the mother of the dead American soldier in the cart; had she received the news yet? The little blond boy on the hospital boat who looked perfectly normal and wanted to live so badly but just died uttering not a word of complaint. The other youngster who died while trying to lie down. The young dying tanker in the forest asking, "Where were you last night?" The face of the young German girl on top of the pile of dead. The German woman minus legs from brutal artillery fire, her face in the mud. All of these faces are etched in my memory and linger with me today after all these years.

Upon arrival back at my unit, I found my battalion preparing to leave Buer to begin security and military government duties in the vicinity of Bad Lippspringe. On May 16, 1945, my battery was relieved from attachment with Provost Marshal XVI Corps Artillery to establish local security in the vicinity of Brakel, Germany. Twenty-four prisoners of war (POWs) were evacuated to Vennebeck on May 16, bringing the total POWs evacuated to 366 and closing all POW camps in the vicinity of Brakel. Our battalion received orders to proceed by motor march to the German Ordnance Proving Ground near Hillersleben to arrive on May 31 for the purpose of calibration. All but thirty-eight rounds per tractor of 4.5 ammunition were turned in to ordnance. Battery C moved from Beverungen and established local security in the vicinity of Brakel. On May 30, the British relieved our battalion of all security and military government duties in the vicinity of Brakel. Calibration previously scheduled for May 31 was canceled by order of the commanding general. Orders were received on May 31 from the commanding general, XVI Corps Artillery, to move to Passau, Germany.

After three days in Passau, we received orders to leave and take a position in Altheim, Austria, to perform further security duty. Since all of our field artillery pieces were turned in, our mode of transport shifted back to rail on the "8 chevaux ou 40 hommes" boxcar. On June 5, we loaded our duffel bags on a waiting train and headed for Altheim, about three hundred miles north. Our required gear at this point was our green work uniforms, steel helmets, and carbine rifles. We rode all night, arriving in Altheim about 11 A.M. on June 6, 1945. D-day had been exactly one year ago. On our trip we passed through a part of Germany that was hardly touched by the war, which included the Black Forest and the area of Berchtesgaden, where Hitler's hideout was located.

There was a feeling of peace and tranquility when contrasted with the Germany we had just left. Upon arrival at the small village of Altheim, we were taken to two large farmhouses where my battery would live. A small creek ran in front of our house; on the other side was an open space of about five acres that was crowded with German prisoners. A low electrical fence bordered this area. The prisoners were in a destitute state with little food and few toilet articles. Commerce between the prisoners and the guards quickly began. We traded K rations, butter and bread, cigarettes, and chocolate bars for German pistols and various trinkets and souvenirs. They had been our bitter, faceless enemies on the battleground, but now they simply appeared human in their quest for basic necessities for survival. After discovering their desperate need for food, I found myself trading K rations for things I did not need or want, just so that they could have something to eat. For some reason, the fact that some of them had committed atrocities mattered little at the time—maybe because I already knew that they would all somehow pay for their crimes.

We stood guard all night and made regular rounds of the perimeter of the compound. About halfway down one side of the compound was a shallow drainage ditch leading under the wire fence and out of the compound. The drainage ditch was approximately two feet deep and about four feet wide. Grass was all around the ditch in an effort to prevent erosion as the water flowed through. At night I would occasionally check with guards at different points to be sure they were alert in the early morning hours. There were no lights around the compound, so security guards carried flashlights. I noticed that on some mornings, the grass in the bottom of the ditch was flat, but I assumed that it was from the rain—some nights it rained hard enough for the water to rise six to eight inches in the ditch. One night, however, while making my rounds, I happened to shine my light toward the drainage ditch and saw a flash. It was a reflection of the steel plate that German soldiers had around the heel of their combat boots. I discovered a German prisoner trying to escape. He was about fifteen feet outside the compound and the fence. He jumped up, ran toward me, and yelled, *"Nicht schiessen!"* (Don't shoot). I directed him to lie down, and another guard searched him for a weapon. He was then taken to the compound headquarters and reported as "trying to escape." I discovered that the reason the grass was flat was that prisoners had been escaping at night.

Three weeks after our arrival in Altheim, a tank company was assigned to assist us on security duty two nights a week. On one night when the tankers were on duty, a prisoner was caught about twenty feet outside the fence line. The tanker killed the attempted escapee while he was lying down without even giving him the opportunity to get up. I disagreed with the policy of the tankers. Even though it was legal to kill a prisoner attempting to escape, the war was over, and these prisoners were desperate men just trying to find food and return home. The tankers were later relieved of security duty in Austria. We remained in Altheim for another six weeks, and the security duty became routine.

On July 14, our battalion received orders to move somewhere in southern France. We cleaned up our housing and all the surrounding area, washed our clothes, and prepared for our journey across Europe. Only the people who owned the house we lived in came to say good-bye. The morning of July 16, we mounted the railcars and headed for southern France. By sunset we reached the site of Hitler's Berchtesgaden. Our train stopped to refuel, so we unloaded to stretch our legs and look around. Berchtesgaden is located on the top of a mountain and was commonly referred to as the "Eagle's Nest." There were five or six German teenage girls at the small train station. Two of them came over and explained what the Eagle's Nest was all about. They pointed out the ledge that extends out from the house—from this ledge you can look out over four countries.

By this time it was dark, and the red light on the last car of the train was all I could see. Keep in mind that when we got off the train, it was for just a few minutes, so we did not have our helmets or carbines. I was talking with the girls and heard someone call me from the train saying it was time to go. I said, "I'll be right there." Someone called a second time saying the train was leaving. There was another chief of section with me, and as we turned and looked toward the train, all we saw were red lights of the end car moving away. We immediately started running toward the train and got to within about five feet of the end car when we stumbled and fell. We both ended up on the ground as the train picked up speed and pulled away. Neither of us had our helmet or gun, and it was against the law for a soldier to be drifting around unarmed. We also had no knowledge of where the train was going.

There was a highway about a half mile west of the railroad tracks. We decided to get to the highway and attempt to catch a ride in the same direction as the railroad tracks. A truck came by about 9:30 P.M. and gave us a ride to the next city, which was Munich. We arrived in Munich about 4:00 the next morning. Our greatest fear was being arrested by the army military police for being improperly dressed. The wee hour of the morning saved us. I inquired at the station if a trainload of soldiers had been through. It had not, and the station was only a barely operating bombed-out shell. We went back to the highway to try to get a ride to the next city—Augsburg. A truck picked us up at about 4:45 and dropped us off at about 8:30 at a point near the train station. We walked over to the station and waited to see if the train would come through. At about 9:00 A.M., I saw a train in the distance. As it approached, I saw a soldier from Battery A standing beside the train door. I knew then that we had made it and caught up with our train. We had missed the train at about 9:30 the previous night, followed the highway that always remained near the railroad tracks, and found the train around 9:30 the next morning. I had never been happier to see a train.

We rode the train all day and night and arrived at Marseilles, France, the morning of July 18. In Marseilles we were assigned to single-story barracks with a common shower located in the center of the barrack. After getting settled, the first thing I wanted to do was take a shower. I stayed under the shower for about twenty minutes, and as I walked out the exit door, I met my brother Charles coming into the shower. I had not seen him since early 1942 when he was sent off to war in North Africa with the 23rd Division. I could not believe my eyes. We spent only a few minutes together because my fallout meeting was to begin in fifteen minutes. I did not see him again as a soldier.

I knew our fallout meeting was important because it was about the breakup of the 777th Field Artillery Battalion. The war in Japan was still going on, but the army had a policy that African American combat units were broken up overseas before they got back to the United States. All the ticker-tape parades down Broadway and the troops marching to receive glory from a grateful public were made up of white units. The U.S. public knew nothing about the heroism of the African American troops of the 969th Field Artillery, who helped stop the German attack in the Battle of the Bulge, where during the early phase of the battle many white troops deserted out of fear of the enemy and where the first hanging of a U.S. soldier for desertion in one hundred years took place. It was during this same engagement that the African American battalion, the 333rd Field Artillery, fought to the very end and was nearly demolished by the Germans.

Zelmo

Now a word about my cousin Zelmo. On the misty, cold morning of Saturday, December 16, 1944, some five hundred thousand German soldiers suddenly attacked American forces located in the Ardennes region of Belgium and Luxembourg. (The following discussion of the German counteroffensive relies heavily on Charles Whiting, *Ardennes, the Secret War.*) At exactly 3:30 A.M. on this cold December morning, the complete length of our front suddenly erupted in fire and flame. The weight of artillery from three German armies, ranging from 16-inch railway guns to 3-inch mortars, descended on the startled Americans of the four divisions holding the line. German infantrymen dressed in white uniforms emerged from the forest after blending with the snow, cheering as they moved forward in a half trot. Then the tanks, hundreds of them, began to rumble forward. All of a sudden the firing ceased, and there was a stunned silence as the survivors, with ashen faces and unspoken questions in their wide eyes, attempted to collect themselves. The only sound was that of the enemy's breathing and their boots as they crushed against the frozen ground with each step. Some were almost running as they moved westward. By now it was daybreak, and individual shafts of sunlight were visible on the eastern horizon. It was about 5:30. Then, all of a sudden, the entire horizon lit up as if an atomic switch had been flipped.

It was at this time that the first ghostlike figures in white camouflaged caps began their slow, ominous advance, twenty abreast with their weapons carried at high port. Elements of five U.S. divisions plus support troops fell back in confusion at the German counterattack. Two regiments of the 106th Infantry Division, cut off and surrounded atop the mountainous Schnee Eiffel, surrendered after only brief fighting, the largest battlefield surrender of U.S. troops during World War II. The African American troops of the 333rd Field Artillery Battalion faced the initial onslaught of the German counteroffensive that Saturday morning and were overrun by superior forces. However, Charlie Battery engaged the enemy, killing hundreds before most of them were cremated by enemy rockets in their gun pits.

The number killed, wounded, or captured of the 333rd was so high after it was overrun by the Germans the first day that it was decommissioned as a field artillery unit. The battalion was assigned new duties, such as guarding government installations and documents considered vital to the government and manning roadblocks in strategic places of military interest in Germany.

No one knows what happened to my cousin Zelmo, as he could not be located or identified after the rocket attack on his gun crew. No one is sure how he became a patient in a Veterans Administration mental health facility, and no one knows how and when he escaped the carnage that Saturday morning, December 16, 1944, as there were no immediate reports of the number of survivors. The only thing we know is he is in the Veterans Administration psychiatric ward today, fifty-five years later. He was never well enough to go home.

His brother, Clinton, saw him a year ago as he was standing on the corner of Dowling and Scott Streets in Houston, Texas, a primarily colored neighborhood in the Third Ward. Clinton got within five feet of Zelmo when Zelmo looked around, saw Clinton, and ran. He is an old man now, and he just kept running. His short gray hair was plastered down to his head in the style of his high school class at Smithville Colored High during the 1940s. His neck was scrawny and too small for the collar of his loose clothes. He seemed to have shrunk. The determination we had seen in his eyes of yesteryear was gone. It had evolved into sadness and hopelessness, but he still seemed alert with the quickness of a cannoneer. Clinton said he wore a Veterans Administration hospital uniform and looked very sad. He scarcely recognized him and was surprised to see him, because no one in the family knew where he was. We thought he was killed and unidentified during the German initial assault that Saturday morning. He had not been seen since he went away to the war more than fifty-five years ago. As youngsters, Zelmo, Clinton, and I would sit at the feet of Uncle Anderson, their father and my uncle, and listen to his exploits as a World War I soldier in France. None of us had any idea that a similar fate would ever befall one of us. Unfortunately, Zelmo is a mere shell today. The war imprisoned his mind but left his body whole, and he has been forced to live in this agony since then. What would have helped him come back from the brink of madness? Perhaps nothing; but maybe Zelmo needed what we all did after our terrifying time there—the appreciation and acknowledgment from a grateful public of a job well done. The point of all of this is to make known my feelings about the army policy of deactivating African American combat units overseas and not giving them the opportunity to be thanked by a grateful American public.

Although the story of the army experience of two colored Americans setting out with the same objective but with a great divergence in outcomes makes interesting as well as informative reading for the general public, the point of its focus is too sobering and disturbing a story to be considered mere pleasure reading or entertainment. Even though the brutality of the over-running of Zelmo's battery by superior German forces occurred more than five decades ago, the crippling, degenerative way the carnage short-circuited the permanent mental capabilities of young soldiers under stress is a heartbreaking, vivid, and powerful saga that is still pertinent today. This human story has never been told but needs to be; it is indeed a sad one. Zelmo's final life outcome is sort of a mystery. I hope to see and talk to him just once more.

On that gray, gloomy Saturday morning when the world of Charlie Battery and Zelmo fell apart, the top brass played, as described by Charles B. MacDonald in *A Time for Trumpets—the Untold Story of the Battle of the Bulge*. If at the front on Germany's snowbound western border the millions of soldiers, British, French, Canadian, and American, under their command fought and perhaps died that day, they played. After all, it was a Saturday, wasn't it?

The Majdanek Concentration and Death Camp: An Overview

by Elissa Mailänder and Patricia Szobar

PRISONERS' LIVING CONDITIONS

When they arrived at Majdanek, prisoners received colored, triangular pieces of cloth called "chevrons" (*Winkel*) that could be worn in combination to indicate the prisoner's category as designated by the political department. This system of inmate classification was a technique developed by the SS to aid in prisoner surveillance and control. This classification system was also at least nominally successful in achieving an additional objective—that is, to prevent the formation of alliances among prisoners. In April 1942, a system of prisoner numbering was also introduced in Majdanek. A total of 20,000 numbers were assigned in sequence, with new arrivals receiving the numbers previously assigned to their deceased predecessors. The women's camp had a similar numbering system.[1]

The camp consisted of a total of five rectangular fields (*Felder*), each about six hectares in size.[2] Twenty-two barracks stood on each field in two opposite rows. The open space in between was used as a roll-call ground. Here, prisoners assembled twice a day to be counted. It was also here that public punishments were meted out. In addition to the routine daily brutality of the SS troops, the chaotic administration of the camp also had a devastating impact on the day-to-day lives of the prisoners held there. Living conditions in Majdanek were extremely harsh. To borrow the words of a Jewish survivor who described conditions at Majdanek in Eberhard Fechner's documentary:

> There is no one on this earth whose language is adequate to describe what Majdanek was. It was—it is—impossible. Just imagine, one day we heard that some SS troops were at Majdanek looking for people—women—to go to Auschwitz. And we knew that Auschwitz was no bed and breakfast. We knew Auschwitz was a bad place. But we didn't care; we just wanted to get out of where we were.[3]

From its earliest weeks, Majdanek suffered from a water shortage, which contributed to frequent epidemics and outbreaks of disease among the prisoners. According to Wolfgang Scheffler, while the original plan had called for connecting Majdanek to Lublin's municipal water supply, the civilian administration of Lublin had rejected the proposal, arguing that the city could not afford to surrender such a large share of its water supply.[4] Consequently, the camp at Majdanek relied on a single well for all of its drinking water. Further compounding this issue was the well's position immediately adjacent to the latrines and the kitchen. In its initial phase, the women's camp had no latrines. Instead, the female prisoners were forced to relieve themselves in trenches that had been dug behind the barracks.[5] It was not until summer 1943 that a barrack at the end of each field was set up to serve as a washing facility and latrine. Depending on the camp's occupancy, anywhere between 1,000 and 6,000 women shared the use of these facilities at any given time.

In the evenings after curfew, the women were not allowed to leave their barracks. Each barrack had only a single bucket, in which hundreds of inmates were forced to relieve themselves. Given that the meals consisted largely of water (at midday and in the evening, the women typically received turnip or nettle soup, while the morning's meager rations consisted of dandelion coffee), sanitary conditions within the barracks were beyond deplorable. Many of the women, even those not suffering from typhoid, were so weak that it was virtually impossible for them to climb down from the triple-deck bunks and make it to the bucket in time.

Thus, it was not long before the prisoners' barracks became filthy, lice-infested breeding grounds for disease and epidemics. Not surprisingly, the constant fear of disease had the effect of discouraging interaction among the prisoners. Poorly constructed barracks along with a lack of furnishings and other amenities added to the risk of disease.[6] Because each barrack was equipped with only one stove, the women subsisted in near-freezing winter temperatures. By contrast, the wooden frame barracks trapped the summer heat, leaving the women to swelter.

Within just a few months of the camp's establishment, it was clear the high death rate was interfering with the goal of exploiting the prisoners' labor. In March 1942, the WVHA launched its first attempt to improve the disastrous conditions in the concentration camp. In August 1942, the Chief Economic and Administrative Office issued a directive to decrease the mortality.[7] However, because the SS camp administration still retained responsibility for obtaining and distributing food and medications to the inmates, there was essentially no change at Majdanek after this edict. The Majdanek administration made little to no effort to improve food and living conditions for the prisoners, nor did it attempt to interfere with the brutal treatment meted out by the SS guards. Instead, the camp administration employed various ruses to conceal the high mortality rate. For example, in camp log books, the names of deceased inmates would be replaced with those of incoming prisoners whose names had not yet been officially registered. These and other loopholes for manipulating prisoner statistics were common throughout the concentration camp system.

In fall 1942, the WVHA again emphasized its intention to exploit Jewish prisoners for labor. By that time, however, the Jewish prisoners in Majdanek had either died from starvation and disease, or had been shot. Between April and October 1943, various German companies and the WVHA in Oranienburg again attempted to exert influence over camp personnel, and strengthen ties between Majdanek's forced-labor resources and the German armaments industry by expanding the "Osti" factory.[8] However, it was not long before this effort to build an SS economic empire on a foundation of Jewish forced labor faltered.

Catastrophic living conditions and a resultant high mortality rate, however, were not only a result of poor facilities, misadministration on the part of the WVHA, and negligence on the part of the camp commandant and camp compound leader.[9] In reality, the camp guards held sway over much of the day-to-day lives of prisoners within the various camps that made up Majdanek, as well as the various labor detachments in which prisoners worked. By way of their brutality, the female guards and the male SS troops greatly exacerbated the prisoners' already precarious circumstances. For example, the *Aufseherin* Hildegard Lächert distributed ballroom dresses, children's sweaters, and high-heeled shoes to new arrivals, even though the camp was well-supplied with the practical clothing, shoes, and other items necessary for daily camp life (all of which came from the camp's storehouses, stacked high with possessions taken from new arrivals).[10] In other words, this unsuitable clothing was distributed not out of necessity, but rather with the intention of making life even more difficult for the prisoners. As it was, given the living and work conditions at Majdanek, being forced to wear inadequate clothing was very much a life-threatening ordeal.

In the Nazi racial hierarchy, the various categories of prisoners were not equal. Within this system, "Aryan" German and Austrian inmates occupied the top of the hierarchy, followed by Northern and Western Europeans. Next came Czechs, Poles, Russians, and Soviet prisoners of war, all deemed "racially inferior." At the bottom of the hierarchy were the Jewish prisoners and the Sinti and Roma. However, even within a particular category, the inmates were not all equal. As a rule, prisoner-functionaries (*Funktionshäftlinge*) were granted a slightly larger food ration, enjoyed better sanitary conditions, and were exempted from the most grueling manual labor. The prisoner-functionaries, therefore, occupied a visible position, symbolized by a special arm-band that identified them within the forced prisoner community. A functionary position also entailed working in direct cooperation with the SS, whether on the camp grounds, in administrative offices, or on labor detachments. Functionary posts offered a position of comparative prominence within the forced society of prisoners, including a better chance at survival and a degree of decision-making authority over fellow inmates. However, these advantages came with the burden of helping to enforce the will of the SS. The rights and privileges accorded to prisoner-functionaries, including their power over other prisoners, could take a variety of forms. This special status, in turn, could spell the difference between survival and death for their fellow inmates.[11]

Notes

1. Kranz, "Zeittafel," 210.
2. Testimonies specifically use the term field and therefore I decided to remain true to the original source language instead of using the arguably more accurate translation of area or section.
3. Anonymous female Jewish survivor, in Eberhard Fechner, *Norddeutscher Rundfunk: Der Prozess: Eine Darstellung des Majdanek-Verfahrens in Düsseldorf* (video cassettes; 1984), part 1.
4. Wolfgang Scheffler, in Fechner, *Der Prozess*, part 1.

5. Testimony by Rywka Awronska from 15 February 1978, main hearing, HStA Düsseldorf, Ger. Rep. 432 No. 282, p. 10 (Dieter Ambach and Thomas Köhler, eds. *Lublin-Majdanek. Das Konzentrations- und Vernichtungslager im Spiegel von Zeugenaussagen*, vol. 12, *Juristische Zeitgeschichte* [Dusseldorf, 2003], 104).

6. On the barracks, see Axel Dossmann, Jan Wenzel, and Kai Wenzel, *Architektur auf Zeit. Baracken, Pavillons, Container* (Berlin, 2006).

7. See Hermann Kaienburg, "Vernichtung durch Arbeit." *Der Fall Neuengamme. Die Wirtschaftsbestrebungen der SS und ihre Auswirkungen auf die Existenzbedingungen der KZ-Gefangenen* (Bonn: Dietz, 1990).

8. Pohl, *Von der "Judenpolitik" zum Judenmord*, 181.

9. See chapter 5 of this work.

10. According to testimony by a Majdanek survivor, in Fechner, *Der Prozess*, part 1.

11. See Bernhard Strebel, "Verlängerter Arm der SS oder schützende Hand? Drei Fallbeispiele von weiblichen Funktionshäftlingen im KZ Ravensbrück," *WerkstattGeschichte* 12 (1995): 35–49.

Questions for Reflection

These Perspectives excerpts take us to some of the most unforgettable places of the 20th century: a first-hand account of the Hitler youth organizations, the gripping experience of an African-American soldier in WWII, and the role of female concentration camp guards. As you reflect on how these and other individuals handle their brush with history, answer the following questions.

1. What two Hitler youth organizations are discussed in the first excerpt? What did they revolve around? What do you think their attraction was? Were the youth brainwashed?

2. What were *Geländespiele*? What role did film play in the organizations?

3. In the second excerpt, who was Zelmo? What major battle is being discussed at the beginning of the excerpt? Describe the sacrifice of the Charlie Battery.

4. What happened to Zelmo? How is this experience used by the author to make a point about the first-hand experience of WWII? What is that point?

5. The Majdanek concentration camp is the focus of the last excerpt. Where was Majdanek located? What was the purpose of the classification system used at Majdanek?

6. Describe the prisoners' conditions and routine. Who was *Aufseherin* Hildegard Lächert? From what is said about her, what can you gather about the role of SS women at this camp? Are you surprised that women were part of the SS administration and the "workaday violence" of the camps?

7. Describe how in each of the cases noted in the excerpts above ordinary individuals were caught up in momentous events. What about the excerpts themselves makes interpreting them relatively easy or difficult?

8. Sometimes "history" is personified and events of the past are cast as a powerful current that sweeps up innocent people to do terrible things. Others stress that people make

situations, that even the lowliest functionary in a great historical drama always has a choice. What do you think?

Activities Menu

Your instructor may assign one or more of the following learning activities:

Prewriting Exercise

Take a minute and write a paragraph (half page of notebook paper) on what you know about Nazi youth organizations.

Media

Select a relevant video program from one of the following and write a one-page (double-spaced) reaction.

- TED Talk
- Munk Debates
- C-SPAN
- Crash Course

Source Search

Select and read two related primary sources found online at the Modern History Sourcebook and incorporate them into your essay.

Short Essay I

Write a three-page (double-spaced) essay of about 750 words in answer to the following question: Drawing on the material from this chapter, write a short wartime sketch of Zelmo. In what ways did he represent the black soldier's WWII experience?

Short Essay II

Write a three-page (double-spaced) essay of about 750 words in answer to the following thesis. Defend or refute: "Hitler youth and female SS guards at Majdanek can't be held responsible for their associations and actions. They were just part of their culture and context at the time."

Role-Playing Exercise

Have three students assume the roles of individuals in this chapter: a member of the Hitler youth organization, a black soldier in WWII, and a female concentration camp guard. Each student should give a first-hand account of what they saw and experienced—especially the dilemmas they faced.

Quiz

Complete a quiz created by your instructor.

Suggested Reading

Leon Goldensohn, *The Nuremberg Interviews* (2005)

Elissa Mailänder and Patricia Szobar, "The Majdanek Concentration and Death Camp: An Overview," in *Female SS Guards and Workaday Violence: The Majdanek Concentration Camp, 1942-1944* (2015)

James H. Madison, *World War II: A History in Documents* (2009)

Emiel W. Owens, "In Battle in Europe," in *Blood on German Snow: An African American Artilleryman in World War II and Beyond* (2006)

Frederic C. Tubach, "Jungvolk and Hitler Youth," in *German Voices: Memories of the Life During Hitler's Third Reich* (2011)

Chapter 7

Chapter Skill	Developing a Persuasive Argument
Chapter Issue	Ideology & Power
Chapter Objectives (Students will...)	• Identify three specific ways in which ideology has shaped power in the 20th century • Assess three current perspectives on ideology and power in the 20th century • Demonstrate in a short essay on ideology and power the ability to develop a persuasive argument
Assignments and Assessments	1. Read the Setup Narrative 2. Listen to the Lecture(s) 3. Read the Perspectives excerpts 4. Compose a three-page Essay in answer to the assigned prompt

Setup Narrative: Ideology & Power

In Chapter 6 we looked at the impact of political realignments in the early 20th century. In this chapter, we turn our attention to the ideological realignments of the past century. How did the home of the Renaissance become that of Mussolini's Blackshirts? How did the land of the Reformation become the indelible symbol of antisemitism and genocide? How did allies in two world wars—the U.S. and Russia—become enemies in another kind of battle in peacetime, the Cold War? Ideas matter, so do institutions. After ideology married power, the human family was never the same.

The 20th century was a century of ideas. Science, the humanities, politics, art, and music—all were revolutionized by new theories. Some of these theories were turned into ideals, and some of these ideals became ideologies that held sway over millions globally. As we look back over the past two centuries, they are filled with "-isms." The 19th century? Romanticism, conservatism, liberalism, capitalism, socialism, Marxism, imperialism, and nationalism. The 20th century? Communism and fascism were added to the list. How do we understand this penchant for "-isms"? And how can we assess these ideologies, especially in relationship to the power that most of them seemed to exert over populations at home and abroad?

First, a few definitions. The dominant economic system across the globe since about 1600 is capitalism, a system that employs private (as opposed to state or "public") capital markets for corporate organization, investment, finance, and personal assets. The great nemesis of capitalism was communism, but here an important distinction is necessary: socialism, Marxism, and communism are not synonymous. Marxism is one type, one variety of socialism, and socialism and communism are distinct. Socialism is an economic system of private property and private ownership governed by public regulation and often by public involvement in the commanding heights of the economy. Aspects of socialism can be found in many governments. Communism has never existed anywhere. Wait a minute, you say, what about the Soviet Union, China, Cuba, Vietnam, etc.? All of these are attempts to put utopian Marxist theory into practice, and in that theory, communism is the ultimate, utopian stage of socialism that is stateless, classless, and distributes economic benefits fairly and evenly. No country has achieved this. In practice, every attempt at a communist society has ended in authoritarian government. Whether this is of the essence of communism or not is a matter of debate. The last "-ism" is the most difficult to define. Attempting to define fascism has twisted students and teachers into pretzels. For what it's worth, my definition is that fascism is a stridently nationalistic, authoritarian state geared for war, supported by a military–industrial complex.

But these definitions, as useful as they may be (and I certainly hope they are), are only part of the picture. Capitalism is as capitalism does, same with socialism, communism, and fascism. In other words, until we take a look at specific case studies, we're stuck in the ethereal, rarified realm of theory. The 20th century gave us several painfully unmistakable cases of each of these ideologies. What's important is that they were always tied to the pursuit of aggrandizing power. When the Bolsheviks took control of the broad, popular soviet movement in 1917 in the name of a communist future, they were taking control of the reigns of the revolution and its future government. When Stalin started playing pontiff with the Russian Communist Party, he began to control the state that party controlled. The same could be said for his contemporaries Mussolini and Hitler. Moreover, WWII added another dimension to the relationship between ideology and power—patriotic defense of the homeland. At war's end, truly heroic sacrifice had become synonymous with the patriotic defense of the *ideology* of homeland. In this context, it's no surprise that a new kind of war was in the offing—especially when nuclear weapons and the fear they created were added to the equation. In fact, fear may be the critical, hidden element in this relationship between ideology and power.

All this is to suggest that the roots of the Cold War lay deep in the story of the West, below and behind the postwar security calculations of the United States and the Soviet Union, as important as those were. Our conceptions of East Asia, the Middle East, Latin America, Africa, and of each other were colored by the psychology inherent in the modern West's marriage of ideology and power. Deeper contradictions in the Soviet system became untenable by the early 1980s, and the fall of the Berlin Wall was memorably emblematic of the end of the era of ideology, or was it? As the excerpts below indicate, this great power, geopolitical competition was a great game that reached all the way down to local school boards and beyond the collapse of communism.

Lecture

Pay attention to the chapter lecture(s), either online or in class.

Tips on Developing a Persuasive Argument

- Nothing is more important in your education than learning to develop a persuasive argument. I know it sounds like hyperbole, but trust me, this skill makes all the difference. Take the time to do it well. If you're not persuaded, your reader or audience won't be either.
- Evidence. Not hearsay, nor conjecture, nor opinion, but clear, firm evidence. Have at least two pieces of solid evidence for every point you make. Three is better, four is best because it gives you the chance to work in some nuance.
- Organization. A persuasive argument is organized, plain and simple. Work as hard on this as getting your information.
- Transitions. Your transitions from one point to the next, or from paragraph to paragraph, are critically important. Make them smooth. You are taking the reader on a trip with you. Let them know when you are about to make a sharp turn.
- Alpha and Omega. No two parts of your argument are more important than your introduction and conclusion. Make them crystal clear. You may think that your copious content will make your case for you. Not true. And remember, your conclusion is not (or not just) a summary—it should be a final, compelling statement of your insights. If you've got some zingers up your sleeve, use them here.

Women Arise: The Red Threat on the Domestic Scene

---

by Mary Brennan

Finally, some anticommunists looked on a broader level at national organizations and the media, which they felt led parents and children astray. Distrusting outsiders in general, anticommunist activists feared the national boards of even such homey institutions as the PTA [Parent Teacher Association] had been subverted by communistic ideas. Numerous newsletters throughout the 1950s and early 1960s warned parents of the dangers hidden in the bulletins and directives issued by the PTA's National Congress. One appalled parent argued that some of the material distributed by the PTA would turn readers into "suitable citizen[s] for atheistic Communism's world government." Another activist called the PTA information kits "Brainwash Study groups" and applauded her community's ability to ignore the "[r]ules laid down by the National Congress."

Others charged that the national PTA officers' "unorthodox and highhanded management . . . Socialist orientation in domestic and foreign affairs, and the hypocrisy of hiding PTA's political motives under the caption 'child welfare' " threatened to ruin the entire organization.[1]

To counter this threat, anticommunist leaders encouraged parents, and members of the community in general, to become more actively involved in their schools. Bella Dodd, a "truly reformed communist," according to Helen Corson of Alerted Americans, warned members of the Barren Hill, Pennsylvania, PTA that "Communists have infiltrated education at all levels." The solution, she told the parents, was to rely more on "local common sense than on advice from the top." In other words, parents had to be responsible for their children's education and guard against insidious influences even in the classroom. The Minute Women agreed. In their national newsletter they reprinted an article by John Crippen, praising his town's success in avoiding struggles with the school board. He explained that the parents "met frequently with our educators"; thus, all were of the same mind-set. He announced that "the National Education Association and many of its departments stand indicted in the court of public opinion." He implied that only the efforts of individuals acting within their communities could stall the spread of socialism.[2] Audrey Plowden, a contributor to *The Spirit,* also agreed. She encouraged parents to "start your own educational program at home." This would "counteract or neutralize the liberal education" promulgated by the public schools and turn children into mini-anticommunist crusaders. "Consider the odds," she wrote. "One teacher, 10 informed conservatives. . . . Start today to turn the tide through the leaders of tomorrow, our children."[3]

Worries about the state of education troubled both male and female anticommunists. Both genders participated in efforts to retain control of their children's education and to keep progressive and communistic ideas away from the schools. Sometimes men organized and led the crusades; sometimes women did. Women played a crucial role in the education struggles in Houston, Los Angeles, and other areas. Their strength could be measured by the level of fear they aroused. In both cities, conservative groups succeeded in unseating school officials accused of having leftist ties. These victories galvanized activists to make further attacks on teachers, newspapers, and local politicians. No one in Houston or Los Angeles doubted that these women had power. Similarly, no one seemed to doubt that they had any right to be involved in this issue.

Obviously, then, female anticommunists actively participated in the battle against the encroachment of communism at home. Believing wholeheartedly in the cause, they searched for any evidence that communists might be making headway in undermining the American way of life. They appeared not to recognize any areas as off-limits to their investigation. Like their male colleagues, they looked for Red influences in politics, economics, education, entertainment, and the arts. They might have deferred to men as spokespersons or leaders, but they also assumed that their own actions played an important role in protecting their homes and families.

Male anticommunists seemed to appreciate women's efforts for the cause. They welcomed female help in letter writing, organizing petitions, hosting fund-raisers and educational meetings, showing up at protests and demonstrations, and performing clerical duties. They sometimes condescendingly acknowledged that women's participation was essential to keep the communists away. Usually, they praised women's actions but described the women themselves as housewives or household managers or mothers. In some ways, they appeared to treat women as one more tool to be used in the crusade against communism.

What neither the men nor the women seemed to see was that women's actions shaped the way anticommunism was perceived by the general public. Through their newsletters, club memberships, rallies, and letter drives, anticommunist women succeeded in educating and then mobilizing large numbers of previously inactive citizens. Their persistence transformed suburban housewives into political operatives. They might have willingly deferred to male politicians on occasion, but in their everyday activities women made the key decisions. Club presidents and advisory boards decided on speakers and projects; individual women mounted campaigns and led letter drives to remove individuals they found suspicious. They might have appeared to accept the domestic ideal, but their actions redefined it at every turn.

In encouraging women to join their political effort, activist women utilized anticommunist rhetoric to explain many of the social challenges of the day. It was far easier for many middle-class white Americans to think of the emerging Civil Rights Movement in terms of communist subversion than to acknowledge the persistence of racism. The ramifications of middle-class women choosing to work to increase their families' consumption of material goods appeared too frightening and far-reaching for a society that professed to hold to an ideal of female domesticity. It was better to blame the communists for seducing women into the workforce. Fearful of an education system that might invite students to challenge the existing value structure, Americans saw the Red menace rather than intellectual enlightenment. Conservative Republicans in particular found this strategy useful in their quest to gain political power. Democrats and even moderate Republicans, they argued, were, perhaps unconsciously, allowing communistic-socialistic influences to transform the U.S. government from its Christian, democratic roots into a sinister clone of the Soviet Union. Obviously, right-wingers emphasized, these fellow travelers must be stopped.

Using anticommunism to further a broader right-wing agenda proved an effective tool for conservative anticommunist women. Since the American public saw communism as a great evil, they accepted women's participation in the fight to stop it. If, then, communism posed not just a political challenge but a social one as well, this expanded the area of women's political involvement. Women could become more embedded in the political system in ways that seemed "normal" to the vast majority of the public. Additionally, women's efforts helped expose the U.S. electorate to the goals and rhetoric of the broader conservative movement. Women became key players in the evolution of the Right.

Notes

1. To editor, n.d., reprinted in *The Farmer's Voice* II, no. 3 (December 1958), Reel 48 F13; "PTA," and "Should PTA Be Abolished?" Special Education Supplement, *The Spirit*, July–August 1964[?], Reel 8 A49, both in Right-Wing Collection.
2. Mrs. Philip Corson, "How to Fight Communism," April 1955, *Alerted Americans*, Reel 13 A73; John K. Crippen, "And Now 'McCallism,'" *The Minute Women of the USA, Inc.*, newsletter, November 1952, Reel 76 M19, both in Right-Wing Collection.
3. Audrey Plowden, "As the Twig Is Bent," *American Spirit*, February–March 1965, Reel 8 A49, Right-Wing Collection.

Authoring a Coup: Iran, 1953

by Hugh Wilford

To be sure, Kim Roosevelt shared in the dominant American view that Iran was dangerously vulnerable to Soviet influence. *Arabs, Oil, and History* portrays the country's political institutions as fragmented and weak, and his later account in *Countercoup* depicts Mosaddeq (inaccurately) as in "alliance ... with the Soviet Union." Yet neither of these works ever conveys the sense of intense, ideological anticommunism detectable in statements by other US Middle East hands from the early Cold War—Loy Henderson, for example, or, for that matter, Archie Roosevelt. Other factors, of a cultural and psychological rather than political nature, seem to have been more important in shaping Kim's behavior toward Iran.[1]

To begin with, there was Roosevelt Anglophilia. Although again not quite as pronounced as in Archie's case, there was a palpable sense of cultural identification between the upper-class British spies who conceived of Operation BOOT and the patrician American who eventually carried it out. "Kim Roosevelt was quickly seen as an important ally in our plans," wrote the MI6 Tehran station chief Monty Woodhouse, an Oxford-educated classicist and future baron. "Like his grandfather, and also his father, he had a natural inclination for bold and imaginative action, and also a friendly sympathy with the British." Family connections doubtless played their part: when Kim passed through London, he tended to stay at the Chester Square residence of the Herberts, the aristocratic British family into which his aunt, Belle's sister Elizabeth, had married. Another of Belle's trans-Atlantic connections was the Duchess of Devonshire, Lady Mary Alice Gascoyne-Cecil ("Moucher" to Belle and other intimates), whose brother Robert ("Bobbety"), Fifth Marquess of Salisbury, was a Conservative Party grandee and, at the time of the Iran coup, acting foreign secretary. There were, admittedly, some strains in the intelligence dimension of the "Special Relationship": perhaps mindful of the recent exposure of Soviet moles—Kim Philby's accomplices Guy Burgess and Donald Maclean—Kim Roosevelt was reluctant to divulge the identity of the CIA's principal BEDAMN agents to his MI6 counterparts, while the latter could not hide "a faint note of envy ... that the Agency was better equipped in the way of funds, personnel, and facilities than was SIS." Overall, though, the CIA's collaboration with MI6—"our cousins," as Kim tellingly referred to the British in *Countercoup*—was conspicuously harmonious, so much so that it was immediately seen as a precedent for future joint operations. "The lesson here is clear," concluded Donald Wilber's CIA report on AJAX, which drew heavily on briefings with Kim Roosevelt. "As in the larger world picture, U.S.–U.K. interests and activities must be coordinated."[2]

If culture helped make Kim receptive to the plans of the British, it set him against Iranians. Despite his affinity for the Arab world, Kim, much like Archie in this regard, viewed Persia through an Orientalist prism inherited from the British. His description of Mosaddeq in *Countercoup* went through the checklist of supposed Oriental character flaws: deviousness, inconsistency, and emotionalism. The "wily" prime minister "was like an ill-tempered, erratic old peasant, … judging all problems from his emotional standpoint," wrote Kim, ignoring Mosaddeq's aristocratic background and European education. "His great strength lay in his ability to mesmerize crowds," the description continued. "His wild exaggerations … led his listeners into almost insane hysteria." Hence Kim, who not much earlier had hailed Arab nationalism as a spontaneous, potent force in its own right, now dismissed its Iranian equivalent as irrational and susceptible to manipulation—exactly the British view of the same phenomenon.[3]

The main exception to this Orientalist representation of Iranians in *Countercoup* was Kim's portrayal of the shah. Whereas in the run-up to the coup many Western observers perceived the vacillating young king as a "mesmerized rabbit," to quote Monty Woodhouse, Kim in contrast portrayed him as a rather heroic figure, on one occasion bravely foiling an assassination attempt, on another piloting a crippled plane to safety, and fleeing Iran in August 1953 not out of cowardice but rather in a premeditated move to stimulate popular anti-Mosaddeq feeling. Yet it seems that this image of the shah was constructed after the fact. At the time of the coup, Kim was no less impatient with the king than other Westerners, at one point threatening to quit Iran "in complete disgust unless the Shah took action within a few days." Moreover, Kim's claim in *Countercoup* that the shah had left "a lasting impression" on him when they first met during his 1947 Middle Eastern tour is belied by the fact that the king is barely mentioned in the 1949 *Arabs, Oil, and History*. Interestingly, this process of reinventing the shah as a more decisive, virile, Western-like leader seems to have begun immediately after the August 19 coup, when Loy Henderson described him to Washington as showing newfound "vigour, decision, and clear thinking," and Kim called him "a new man."[4]

The argument here is not that Kim Roosevelt staged the 1953 coup because he disliked Iranians. Rather, it is that, as for other Anglo-American observers at this time, Orientalist attitudes clouded his judgment of Persian politics and encouraged his tendency to view Iran as a place for personal adventure, a playing field for spy games. This last impulse, which for Kim was strongly associated with his identity as a Roosevelt man, is evident throughout the narrative of events offered in *Countercoup*. As Kim set off from Beirut for Iran in July 1953, for example, he remembered what his father, Kermit, "wrote of his arrival in East Africa with *his* father, T.R., in 1909 on *The African Game Trails* trip. 'It was a great adventure, and all the world was young!'" The implicit comparison of TP-AJAX to one of his father's or grandfather's hunting expeditions was reinforced by "the traditional French hunter's sendoff" that Kim received from a Lebanese friend. The connection to earlier Roosevelt foreign adventures was not lost on contemporaries. Writing Washing-ton shortly after the coup, the chief of the US military mission to Iran, Robert A. McClure, observed, "Frank W[isner]'s boys did a grand job, and wielded a big stick."[5]

Other incidents described in *Countercoup* add to the impression that Kim regarded his mission to Iran as a Kiplingesque adventure. He entered the country in July not bothering to conceal his identity; he showed his passport to a border guard, who mistakenly recorded his name as one of his distinguishing physical characteristics (a suitably swashbuckling one): "Mr. Scar on Right Forehead." On August 19, he belatedly responded to Walter Bedell Smith's cable ordering his return home, explaining that the tide had just turned in the shah's favor and then cheekily signing off, "Love and kisses from all the team." The sense of spying fun-and-games is heightened by the frequent references to actual games, especially card games, that populate *Countercoup*. Even the operation's "theme song," a tune Kim played repeatedly in the weeks before the coup, was about games: "Luck Be a Lady Tonight," the gambling song from the musical *Guys and Dolls*.[6]

The more one reads Kim's account of TP-AJAX in *Countercoup*, the more one is struck by its resemblance to an adventure novel or spy thriller. There are the allusions to Kipling, both implicit and explicit, as when Kim (Roosevelt) likens some bearded, roaming tribesmen in eastern Iran to Mahbub Ali in *Kim* (the novel). Then there is the narrative's main framing device, Kim's journey from Washington to Tehran, which both builds suspense and enables him to set the scene for the coup by recounting his previous experience of Iran. *Kim*, too, is basically about a journey that culminates in a decisive play in the Great Game. One also thinks of John Buchan's *Greenmantle* and its hero Richard Hannay's perilous trek across World War I Europe to the novel's climactic battle scene in Turkey.

If *Countercoup* reads like a novel, this was no coincidence: by the time Kim wrote the book in the 1970s, he had been telling the story of Operation AJAX for years. The process of emplotting the chaotic events that had taken place in Tehran, turning them into a coherent story to tell others, began immediately after the coup, when Kim stopped off in London on his way home and met with MI6 officials for debriefing. Both *Countercoup* and Donald Wilber's 1954 report on AJAX are surprisingly frank on this score. "They wanted the whole story, ... concentrating on the glamorous features of the operation," Kim wrote of his meetings with the British spies, who clearly viewed Mosaddeq's removal as an opportunity to improve their standing with the Foreign Office. Kim obliged by telling his tale over dinner at the grill room of the Connaught Hotel "as elaborately and excitingly as [he] possibly could," including "all the names and numbers of the players, every suspicion, hope or anxiety [he] had known." The following day, with his "routine down cold, in living color," Kim visited the Foreign Office, where, as requested by his friends in MI6, he gave acting foreign secretary Lord Salisbury (Moucher's brother Bobbety) "the full treatment": "a vivid account of the recent disturbances in Iran," as Salisbury himself described it after the meeting. According to the Wilber coup report, Salisbury "appeared to be absolutely fascinated." As he left the Foreign Office, Kim encountered an MI6 official clutching "a folder covered with red ribbons, sealing wax, and other *objets d'art*" who excitedly told him that the acting foreign secretary had just given the go-ahead to another Secret Service operation he had previously been reluctant to approve.[7]

From the Foreign Office, it was on to the final appointment of the day, at Number 10 Downing Street. Led to a living room by a military aide, Kim found Prime Minister Winston Churchill lying in a bed, propped up by pillows. The old adventurer had recently suffered a stroke and was clearly in bad shape. "He had great difficulty in hearing; occasional difficulty in articulating; and apparent difficulty seeing to his left," so Kim reported after the meeting. Nevertheless, the young American was greeted enthusiastically and instructed to pull up a chair on the right-hand side of the bed. There he sat for the next two hours, telling the story of the coup as the ailing prime minister, "consumed alternately by curiosity and by sleepiness," slipped in and out of a doze. At the tale's end, Sir Winston grinned, shifted himself up on his pillows, and addressed his visitor. "Young man," Kim recalled him saying, "if I had been but a few years younger, I would have loved nothing better than to have served under your command in this great venture." "Thank you, sir," replied Kim, deeply moved by "what was, coming from this man, the supreme compliment." The scene, which resembled nothing so much as a man telling a child a bedtime story, could not have been more poignant: Kim had gotten to rehearse his latter-day enactment of the Great Game narrative for a living relic of Britain's imperial heyday.[8]

The storytelling carried on in America, where Kim now returned, trailing clouds of glory. Fearful of arousing unwelcome press interest by visiting President Eisenhower in his Denver retreat—too "radio active" for the president's "gold-fish-bowl," as he told a British official—Kim spent the last days of August with his family in Nantucket, contenting himself with writing a report for the president that contained personal messages from the shah, General Zahedi, and Prime Minister Churchill. (As in the case of Egypt, it is easy to imagine Kim reveling in the role of personal envoy between kings, presidents, and prime ministers.) The following month, he at last got his chance to tell the president his story in person, presenting a briefing on Operation AJAX at a White House meeting attended by Eisenhower, the Dulles brothers, and other senior figures. "The substance of my report had nothing new," he wrote in *Countercoup*; "it was simply a combination of what I had told our British allies and the story I had given to the dozing Winston Churchill." Nevertheless, the reception was enthusiastic. John Foster Dulles, in particular, "seemed to be purring like a giant cat," Kim observed. The president, too, was impressed but shrewdly noted a literary quality in the reports he was receiving about Iran. They "sounded more like a dime novel than historical facts," he wrote later.[9]

Indeed, this was too good a story to keep completely secret. In the fall of the following year, after another successful CIA coup operation in Guatemala, Allen Dulles authorized Agency cooperation with the *Saturday Evening Post* on a three-part report by Richard and Gladys Harkness, "The Mysterious Doings of CIA." The boosterist story, which appeared around the same time that a presidential commission charged with reviewing the CIA's performance to date reported to the White House, paid particular attention to the "stranger-than-fiction circumstances" in which "the strategic little nation of Iran was rescued from the closing clutch of Moscow." Specific sentences, such as the reporters' insistence that, despite the CIA's enabling role, "the physical overthrow of Mossadegh [sic] was accomplished by the Iranians themselves," sound uncannily like formulations of Kim Roosevelt's—who, it will be remembered, had contributed several articles to the *Saturday Evening Post* before he joined the Agency. Kim, meanwhile, was delighting in telling the tale to guests at his Washington home. Normally a "very quiet, private person," he would, so his son Jonathan recalled later, become quite "garrulous" on the subject of Iran. When the story was published, many retellings later, as *Countercoup*, the intelligence commentator Thomas Powers remarked on the "golly-gee-whiz air" that pervaded the book. It was, he wrote, "the sort of story an old man might set down for the pleasure of his grandchildren," echoing Miles Copeland's observation in *The Game Player* that coups lent themselves particularly well to family storytelling.[10]

The Arab historian Albert Hourani once wrote of T. E. Lawrence and his self-mythologizing memoir of the Arab Revolt, *Seven Pillars of Wisdom*, that Lawrence deliberately acted like an epic hero during World War I and then after the war wrote an epic book about his actions. There was something of this circular, literary quality to Kim Roosevelt's involvement in the Iran coup. His actions were shaped, at least in part, by a cluster of ideas and emotions derived from Roosevelt family lore and earlier literary works. Afterward, indeed even before he had returned home from Iran, Kim was turning the operation into his signature story, his own charge up Kettle Hill or River of Doubt expedition, a real-life Kipling adventure. Others in the CIA (and, for that matter, MI6) encouraged him in this process because it suited their bureaucratic purposes to do so, with the result that the story entered the Agency's own canonical history as one of the signal successes of the Allen Dulles "Golden Era."[11]

If only Kim and his superiors in the CIA had heeded the words spoken by the lama to his fictional namesake in the Kipling novel: "Thou hast loosed an Act upon the world, and as a stone thrown into a pool so spread the consequences thou canst not tell how far."[12]

NOTES

Abbreviations

ABRP	Archibald B. Roosevelt Jr. Papers
ACJP	American Council for Judaism Papers
AR	Archie Roosevelt
AWF	Ann Whitman File
DDEL	Dwight D. Eisenhower Library
DTP	Dorothy Thompson Papers
FAOHP	Foreign Affairs Oral History Project
FO	Foreign Office
FRUS	*Foreign Relations of the United States*
HSTL	Harry S. Truman Library
JFDP	John Foster Dulles Papers
JNP	John Nuveen Jr. Papers
KR	Kermit "Kim" Roosevelt
KRBRP	Kermit Roosevelt and Belle Roosevelt Papers
MC	Miles Copeland
NA	US National Archives, College Park, MD
PRO	UK Public Record Office, Kew, London
RG	Record Group
WAEP	William Alfred Eddy Papers
WCEP	Wilbur Crane Eveland Papers
WHCF	White House Central Files

1. KR, *Countercoup*, 2.
2. Woodhouse, *Something Ventured*, 120; Wilber, "Overthrow," 6; KR, *Countercoup*, 115; Wilber, "Overthrow," 94.

3. KR, *Countercoup*, 2, 77, 85–86.
4. Woodhouse, "Iran, 1950-1953"; Wilber, "Overthrow," 36; KR, *Countercoup*, 59; FO minute, August 24, 1953, FO 371/104570, PRO; KR, "Memorandum of CIA Representative," attached to Walter Bedell Smith to Dwight Eisenhower, no date [late August/early September, 1953], 32, Iran, 1953 through 1959 (8), International Series, Dwight D. Eisenhower Papers as President of the United States, 1952-61 (Ann Whitman File) (hereafter AWF), DDEL.
5. KR, *Countercoup*, 138; McClure to Jackson, September 14, 1953, 73, McClure, Robert, Jackson Papers, DDEL.
6. KR, *Countercoup*, 140, 191, 172.
7. Ibid., 205, 204; Wilber, "Overthrow," 80; Lord Salisbury, Record of Conversation, August 26, 1953, PREM 11/514, PRO; Wilber, "Overthrow," 84.
8. KR, "Memorandum of CIA Representative"; KR, *Countercoup*, 207.
9. J. A. Ford to D. B. Pitblado, September 2, 1953, PREM 11/514, PRO, quoting a letter from KR to William Strang; see KR, "Memorandum of CIA Representative"; KR, *Countercoup*, 209; Dwight D. Eisenhower, *The White House Years*, vol. 1, *Mandate for Change, 1953–1956* (Garden City, NY: Doubleday, 1963), 164.
10. Richard and Gladys Harkness, "The Mysterious Doings of CIA," *Saturday Evening Post*, November 6, 1954, 66, 68; Jonathan Roosevelt interview; Thomas Powers, "A Book Held Hostage," *Nation*, April 12, 1980, 438, 437.
11. Albert Hourani, "The Myth of T. E. Lawrence," in *Adventures with Britannia: Personalities, Politics, and Culture in Britain*, ed. Wm. Roger Louis (Austin: University of Texas Press, 1996), 23–24.
12. Rudyard Kipling, *Kim: Authoritative Text, Backgrounds, Criticism*, ed. Zohreh T. Sullivan (New York: Norton, 2002), 176.

Americanization, Globalization, and the End of the Cold War

by Frank Ninkovich

CULTURE CHANGE, LEADERSHIP, AND THE END OF THE COLD WAR

A detailed explanation of how the normalization of global society was connected to political change in the Cold War is beyond the scope of this book. Obviously, the political walls of the socialist bloc would not have been breached without the existence of Western consumer societies that exposed how little socialist economies had to offer by contrast. But given the enforced separation of systems, the collapse of the Soviet world was not the product of the coercive force of international society; nor was it the result of an irrepressible desire to emulate Western societies, for the Westernization of peoples under communist rule mostly amounted to a disquieting understanding that they were not like the West. Conspicuously lacking, apart from those states in eastern Europe that saw themselves as victims of Russian imperialism, was the political motivation needed to overturn a well-entrenched order that commanded formidable repressive resources. Consequently, instead of looking to mass culture, any explanation of how the Soviet system collapsed must turn to the thinking of socialist political elites who set in motion the system's dissolution. For it was only the elites who were able to convert background changes in international society and in their own jurisdictions into a political about-face that left behind Cold War mindsets. Traditionally, elites have been notoriously averse to dislodging themselves. And yet, remarkably, in this instance a political cave-in of this kind did take place.

A major part of the explanation for this epochal change lies in the shortcomings of Marxist ideology in the face of new global realities. The burgeoning global fascination with mass consumption presented a fundamental challenge to a regime whose system was best suited to running a steady-state economy. Marxism, like liberal economics, had long focused on production and supply rather than consumption and demand. The stunning appearance of consumer societies, something that even the early bourgeoisie had rejected, was an unwelcome surprise to a socialism that through much of its history had practiced a "left asceticism" that sneered at a bourgeois style of consumption that was looked upon as historically atypical and unsustainable. In the limited consideration that he gave to the contours of life after capitalism, Marx envisioned a system that would satisfy basic needs, thus leaving ample time for leisure and cultural activities. This lifestyle would blossom courtesy of the marvelous productive machine bequeathed by the bourgeoisie to their socialist heirs.[1]

But while the machine would remain, the fuel of innovation would vanish. In a postrevolutionary world where there were no longer any competitive pressures to maximize return on capital, the impulse to continuously introduce new products and improve efficiency would not—in point of fact, could not—survive the collapse of a capitalist society. With no more revolutions in productivity and no more new stuff mandated by cutthroat competition, production would be routinized—administered by a bureaucratic "dictatorship of officials" because factories could not run themselves without hierarchical direction. This form of managed society, as Max Weber understood, would effectively stifle any lingering impulses toward innovation. This was a far cry from the image of dynamism that the Soviet model had once projected, whose attractiveness rested on its apparent ability—quite appealing to authoritarian nationalists—to create industrialized societies that could provide the basic necessities but not much else. Marx had been quite vague on the subject of life under communism, but the torpid socialist systems of the second world offered a convincing sneak preview of what one could expect in the worker's utopia.[2]

Powerless to unleash or to stamp out what had once been disdained as commodity fetishism, socialist societies in the late Cold War years imperceptibly internalized an appreciation of consumerism that their leaders thought prudent to appease as best they could. As early as the 1930s, the Soviet regime had sought to introduce a greater element of choice in consumer purchases, and even made available—at a steep price—limited quantities of luxury goods that in future were restricted to the *nomenklatura*. Consumerism also made notable strides during the Brezhnev years, albeit in a very modest way by Western standards. Nevertheless, even during these good times people understood that life was better elsewhere. The widespread popularity of *samizdat* and *tamizdat* underground literature literally spoke volumes about popular interest in Western culture and, by comparison, about the barren soil of Soviet cultural creativity. The treatment of travel as a privilege and reward implied that the grass was much greener on the outside (as those who visited the West quickly found out for themselves), while the large audiences that tuned in to Western radio broadcasts showed curiosity about life in the West and a corresponding cynicism about glowing official descriptions of domestic life under socialism. How many people in the West tuned in to Radio Moscow?

The most telling aspect of this latent consumerism was the public's awareness of being excluded from international society. Take, for example, the growing number of citizens of the USSR who during the closing years of the Cold War expressed the desire to live in "a normal country" as *normalniye lyudi*, that is, normal people. What was it like to live in a normal country? It was to be international, to participate in something that once would have been considered impossible: a cosmopolitan mass culture. There was a long list of standard features of life, to which the rest of the world had grown accustomed, that the Soviet public was aware of not enjoying: pop music, travel and tourism, vibrant literature, entertaining movies and TV programs, and stylish clothing, among other aspects of vigorous mass cultures. Teenagers desired the right to be rebellious and alienated. There was an egalitarian aspect, too, to this dilation of desire and its satisfaction, a democratization of luxury in which the gap between the wealthy and the average man was closed considerably—the practical gap between chic Rolex and lowly Timex was virtually zero. Overall, the quality of life for middle-class individuals in the West had become demonstrably superior to that enjoyed by the upper classes a generation earlier. The Marxist slogan "from each according to his abilities, to each according to his needs" was trumped by a capitalism that promised to fulfill each person's desires.[3]

Whereas the socialist standard of sufficiency had been realized in the USSR in the form of a spartan barracks socialism, the benchmark of consumer civilization turned out to be superabundance, or as Mark Twain once put it, the "limitless multiplication of unnecessary necessities." Consumerism, as Hegel had been among the first to recognize, was "something inexhaustible and illimitable." But, as sociologists have been at pains to reiterate, the kinds of goods promised by a global consumer society were nonessentials: access to art and entertainment, a wardrobe that allowed some enjoyment of fashion, the opportunity to travel, the sampling of varied foods and cuisines beyond the monotonous fare of the local diet and, perhaps most of all, getting a car, which was the most sought-after diploma certifying that one had gained entrée to the good life. Unfortunately for the communist aristocracy, the rise of this new standard in which mere adequacy had become inadequate required an ability to meet expectations of abundance that the regime was abysmally suited, in principle and in practice, to fulfill. By resting their economic appeal on the promise of sufficiency, the Soviets contributed to the alienation of their populace and forfeited any possibility of creating a global background of their own.[4]

Hitherto the long-standing historical tendency in the creation of desire had followed a top-down pattern of cultural transmission. In the diffusion of etiquette, clothing styles, or new standards of beauty like foot binding in China, the arbiters of taste had been aristocrats. Adam Smith, for example, believed, with a touch of Calvinistic disapproval, that much consumption was driven by the desire of commoners to emulate one's aristocratic betters, an assumption that lives on as the rationale behind product endorsements. However, the drivers of consumption were very different in the Cold War world. In mass society, the wellsprings of taste flowed increasingly from the ranks of society itself, from designers, inventors, fashion dictators, jazz musicians, rock performers, and celebrities whose status depended on the ability of markets to materialize their ideas into widely saleable commodities. There was no way that top-down socialist societies could dream of releasing such energies or of commanding them. Whereas the Soviet system excelled at suppressing creative impulses, the bureaucratic architects of the new Soviet man could not command muses for the kind of innovation needed to match the consumer cornucopia of the capitalist West. In a global society in which Calvinist frugality was no longer the norm, recognition was now a matter of keeping up with one's consumerist equals. In this sense, too, international society was egalitarian, though not in the restricted socialist sense of imposed equality. This was a far cry from the socialist prediction that the unification of mankind would come about in the wake of capitalism's globalization of misery. Instead, unification was going forward as a by-product of capitalist abundance.[5]

In addition to the disheartening example of the West, the economic success of a growing number of formerly preindustrial nations also gave life under socialism a lackluster appearance by comparison. For more than a century and a half, spectacular economic growth had been restricted to a small number of early developers in the West. That began to change in the 1970s and 1980s, as Japan, the so-called Asian tigers, and then China joined the globalization caravan. Those societies provided eye-popping contrasts to the arthritic Soviet economic scheme. Their successes also cast doubt on the appeal of anti-imperialism as a global strategy, for their advances were made possible only by participation in a capitalist world economy that, if one were to believe the axioms of the anti-imperialism creed, was bent on squeezing surplus value from dependant peoples.

From a Marxist perspective, there were crucial ideological reasons for taking seriously the global consumer revolution. Though the love affair with consumerism did not stir a primal yearning for democracy, communist leaders as well as traditional elites in countries like France were quick to sense the global political implications. Obviously, the widespread democratization of prosperity made a mockery of the axiomatic Marxist prediction of the inexorable impoverishment of the working class; but in more practical terms, it also challenged the revolutionary strategy of the Soviet Union. The Bolshevik revolution in its beginning phase had been understood by Lenin as a historical anomaly that was explained away by the expectation that revolutions were sure to follow in more developed countries, specifically in Germany. The revolution would be rescued and brought to completion from abroad. When external deliverance failed to materialize, the Stalinist strategy of "Socialism in One Country" resorted to a scheme of self-strengthening in order to guard against the ideologically given likelihood that the capitalist powers would plunge into a fratricidal war that would endanger the USSR.

While World War II validated that analysis, the Cold War did not. Instead of going to war, the first world came closer together; under permissive American hegemony, there were disagreements aplenty, but no fundamental rifts emerged among the capitalist powers. Briefly, salvation from the outside once again seemed possible as hopes were invested in the theory of third world revolution. This idea, whose origins lay in the early Soviet period but which moved to the forefront in the late 1950s, was a conspicuous abandonment of the traditional Marxist idea that revolution would spread outward from the industrialized center. For a time, the vogue of radical third world nationalism confirmed this revision, but it was gainsaid by the proliferation of consumer societies and, as socialist states stumbled economically, by the absence of any effective countermovement against globalization. This posed a theoretical problem: If the revolution would come from neither center nor periphery, where would it come from—Mars? Up to a point, it was easy for Soviet leaders to rewrite history, or to tactically shift ideological course, but the postwar trajectory of events suggested that a complete rethinking of their ideology was in order, which risked forfeiting their identity and reason for being.

The biggest blow to Soviet pride was the defection of China, whose newfound economic dynamism contrasted with Soviet stagnation. The arrival of the People's Republic of China in 1949 had given an enormous boost to the idea that communism was the global wave of the future; but, by the same token, its rancorous departure from the Soviet-led camp in the 1970s consigned the command economy to the bin of old-fashioned ideas. Like the USSR, an initial reliance on bureaucratic administration had transformed the PRC into a formidable power, albeit an impoverished one. Dissatisfaction with Soviet tutelage had already taken a geopolitical turn in Mao Zedong's shift toward a rapprochement with the United States in 1971. That was followed by an even more radical move following Mao's death in 1976, when China switched to a mixed economy that depended on global export markets and massive imports of technology and raw materials.

In pursuit of the so-called Four Modernizations, the nation plugged itself into a world economy whose chief guarantor was the United States. Underscoring the value attached to its participation, China lobbied hard, and successfully, for admission to the newly founded World Trade Organization. The holding of the summer Olympics in Beijing in 2008—a quadrennial pageant seized upon by other former outcast nations as a way of gaining recognition as a respected member of global society— highlighted China's dramatic century-long journey from a geographic expression to a world power and gave the regime a degree of the international respect that it craved. But it also highlighted its membership in the global guild of post-Stalinist modernizers. Ideologically, with some intellectual contortions this turn could be interpreted as a kind of hyper-Menshevism, though whether it had much to do with Marxist theory at all is open to question.[6]

As the most recent of "free riders," China provided the most spectacular example of the gap between globalization and Americanization. The Americanization of China had long been the fond hope of missionary types and China hands from the middle of the nineteenth century through the heyday of the Open Door policies, but Americanization was not on the agenda of the economically supercharged China of Deng Xiaoping. In particular, the brutal suppression of the Tiananmen Square protests in 1989 showed that the Communist Party had no intention of relaxing its political grip. Afterward, the Chinese government took action to prevent the importation of unwelcome American products such as pornography and open access to news from the outside world. By the 1990s, political anti-Americanism began to grow side by side with a cultural nationalism, which showed its face in periodic flare-ups over the future of Taiwan and territorial disputes about unimportant unpopulated islands. Also, China's leaders began to talk about the "cultural security" of their nation, which suggested both a well-founded fear of the cultural by-products of globalization and a shaky understanding of the way that culture and globalization were connected. On the political side, China was often loath to cooperate in the United Nations Security Council and in international climate negotiations.[7]

Nevertheless, despite post-Maoist China's failure to satisfy America's longing to see it democratize, relations were tolerable because it was ruled by the kind of authoritarian regime that the United States had long been able to stomach. Stripped to its bare essentials, China policy was also the premier example of the enduring faith that Americans demonstrated in the beneficent workings of international society over the long term. The way in which the endgame would play out was more readily visible than it had been in the days of containment, when economic integration was an unlikely possibility for socialist societies. US policy makers envisioned the continued blending of China into the world economy and looked forward to the eventual growth of a powerful middle class with liberal leanings to rein in the authoritarian behavior of the regime. Besides, the Chinese economy had become so closely linked to that of the United States that a wholly adversarial relationship was out of the question. This was too much to swallow for some critics who saw international relations in a more threatening light. China's willingness to accept American debt obligations to finance American imports led to the two nations being bound together in what one pundit disparaged as "Chimerica ... an economic monster."[8]

The Soviet Union, meanwhile, was experiencing a "crisis of industrial statism" in which an increasingly sluggish economic engine showed signs of stalling. The objective measures of decline were coupled with a worsening crisis of faith. Marxist ideology had long since left behind the days when it could spur the kind of enthusiasm that had energized the Bolsheviks and the crash programs of industrialization. The mature system was enfeebled by black markets, alienated workers, and an anomie that found expression in rampant alcoholism. Even basic statistical measures on which the regime had long prided itself began to turn down, especially an alarming drop in life expectancy and a stunning decline in the birth rate below replacement levels. After a period of postwar privation, Soviet citizens had become accustomed to a growing standard of living, but by the 1980s, when a demographic crisis showed its face, the formerly tried-and-true expedient of adding more labor inputs was no longer available.[9]

The consumer expectation of more meat in the diet, made possible by grain imports, could no longer be covered by the petro-dollar proceeds from oil exports once prices on the international petroleum market collapsed in the late 1980s. But while it is easy to blame economic ups and downs, the truth is that nothing was working well. In the Soviet imperial borderlands, long-smoldering anti-Russian nationalism showed that the idea of Soviet citizenship was a chimera and that the West, if only for reasons of the grass being greener, was far more attractive. At the same time that the command system was incapable of satisfying the growing material expectations of the population, the official ideology was being hollowed out, setting the stage for a legitimation crisis down the road. For many, Soviet communism was becoming an established religion in which neither the church leaders nor the faithful placed much store. This ideological rot was accompanied by physical decay.

Despite all these gloomy signs, the mixed brew of inchoate dissatisfactions and objective indices of decline found in the Soviet Union of the 1980s did not contain the highly combustible elements needed to set off a revolutionary explosion. The cultural unease in the Soviet Union was less the product of an intense desire to create their own version of the Western good life as it was the product of the understanding that the attributes of the outside world, the normal world, underscored the abnormal character of their own society. This sense of being second-rate was hardly the sensibility expected of the vaunted new "soviet man." Though the intention was to be a model for the rest of the world, Soviet citizens increasingly developed noxious personality traits that traduced the values of the superior human being that the regime was supposed to be creating. But behavior that was openly at odds with the system posed little threat to the regime. The desire for entrepreneurial freedom found expression mostly among black marketers, while the right to dissent was the rallying cry of rebellious, creative, and artistic types, the kinds of people that comprise a small minority in any society. Such popular dissatisfactions as existed were not the stuff of mass revolutionary sentiment. A change of direction, if it was to come at all, would necessarily have to come from above. Thus when the system did finally collapse, it was as if, in the words of one writer, the Russian people had "sleepwalked away from Communism."[10]

For many outside observers then and afterward, social discontents were less a spur to drastic change than the worsening power position of the Soviet Union. In the absence of some kind of far-reaching transformation, Hu Yaobang, the secretary general of the Chinese Communist Party, predicted in 1985 that "the Soviet Union will disappear as a great power in the twenty-first century." Hu's comment to the visiting Richard Nixon reflected a common view that an obsession with national power was the principal consideration in forcing decisions for reform in states like China and the Soviet Union. The ambitious military buildup of the Reagan administration, coupled with heavy investments in new military technologies, threatened to upset the hard-earned power equilibrium by placing enormous pressure on the Soviet command economy to continue supplying both guns and butter. Given that a ruinous proportion of Soviet GDP was already being allocated to military investment, without a dramatic increase in economic growth something would have to give.[11]

If maintaining the power of the USSR had been the principal concern, a logical response to growing American strength would have been to take the wherewithal for military expansion out of the hides of the people, a practice resorted to by despotic regimes throughout history when forced to make a choice. The Soviet version of this kind of politically motivated mobilization would have meant reverting to Stalinist methods of repression and belt-tightening that would have ensured the indefinite continuation of the superpower standoff. Another possibility was for the leadership to kick the can down the road in the hope of muddling through, as many politicos are tempted to do when confronted with chronic problems. The Soviets actually tried this by selecting a few premummified successors to Brezhnev, but they lacked the vitality merely to stay alive, much less to put in motion dramatic change.

Finally, in 1985 the party elite gambled on a dynamic and youthful leader, Mikhail Gorbachev, who was painfully aware that the existing system could not hope to match the West economically and militarily or maintain the pretense of doing so. Gorbachev immediately set about trying to revitalize a sclerotic system by moving toward a mixed market economy under the banner of glasnost and perestroika. Taking advantage of the USSR's top-down system, Gorbachev hoped to stimulate transformational change through a loosening of the state's grip, exactly the reverse of what would have been prescribed by Russian tradition or a Stalinist approach. The extraordinary consequences of his policies—the breakup of the Soviet Union and the end of the Cold War—were wholly unexpected. With someone less venturesome and visionary at the helm, the USSR would have survived indefinitely, as most experts were predicting, and the Cold War might not have ended so peacefully.[12]

Given Gorbachev's historical significance, one needs to ask why he felt compelled to take a series of steps that set in motion the dissolution of the Soviet system, a question that is more pressing as he was by all accounts a socialist true believer. Most likely it was precisely his beliefs that hold the key to understanding his moves. Here was a man who was motivated not by apparatchik careerism but by the pained recognition that the operative ideology of the USSR had drifted far away from its mooring in fundamental beliefs, much as the pre-Reformation church had lost touch with its core convictions. Gorbachev easily passed one test of the genuineness of an ideology: the willingness of its true believers to take action when current practices no longer express basic principles, which is why disillusioned ideologues often make the best realists. More Loyola than Luther, he had no intention of precipitating the collapse of the USSR, but he understood that continuing, like some conditioned trail horse, to plod along the same path as his predecessors would only make a bad situation intolerable. Given the long-term prospects for a Soviet slide into irrelevance, Gorbachev felt compelled to initiate drastic reforms before the point of no return had been reached. Opening wide the political floodgates might wreak some havoc downstream, but at least it would relieve the buildup of pressures that would prove disastrous if nothing were done. Continuing to temporize would also be to say goodbye to the receding prospect of rescuing the humanistic promise of socialism. On one occasion he put the urgency of the need for radical change in terms reminiscent of Rabbi Hillel: "If not us, then who? If not now, when?"[13]

In an information-poor society, Gorbachev's panoramic vantage point enabled him to better grasp the big picture of troubles that ordinary citizens experienced as a vague cultural unease. Much of his dissatisfaction came from the recognition that the USSR was out of step with the march of events and the spirit of the age. More than any other political leader of his day, he was able to look with fresh eyes past the day-to-day predicaments of politics to the deeper long-term implications of the recasting of the global setting wrought by globalization. Conventional political thinking, he knew, was badly out of step with the *longue durée*. Though he continued to cling to the hope of socialism as an ultimate solution, he understood that the supposed vanguard nation had dropped out of history's line of march. In contrast to American policy, where the connection to a brighter future was implicit, the ideology of the USSR was explicitly yoked to the expectation that globalization would bring universal misery to the workers of the world. As a fallback, neo-Marxists had resorted to theories of mass society, ideological hegemony—domination of culture by the ruling classes—and condemnation of the "culture industry" to explain the delay in the creation of a global proletariat that was conscious of itself as the universal class. But given the emergence of a firmly established cultural background of consumerism throughout the world, Gorbachev foresaw no prospect of an "Aha!" moment when the ideological scales would fall from the eyes of deceived workers. His retrospective description of the Soviet experiment minced no words: "from the historical point of view it was a dead end in social development." World history, he realized, had taken a different direction.[14]

Like his fellow citizens, Gorbachev understood that this was a world in which the Soviet system was not normal and had no prospect of becoming so. Despite mixed feelings about the "major changes that had occurred in the most fundamental aspects of daily life during the years after World War II," there was no longer any place for the Soviet Union's brand of socialism. Consequently, there was no choice but to come to terms with "the internationalization of economic and then of all social life" by internalizing the reality of global society. This meant rejoining the world pretty much on the world's terms. In his words, the USSR needed "to live in harmony with mankind's universal values, abide by the norms of international law, follow the 'rules of the game' in our economic relations with the outside world," including membership in the flagship institutions of globalization, the World Bank and the IMF. In his Nobel lecture, Gorbachev underscored the point: "we have to carry out measures that would enable us really to open up to the world economy and become its organic part." The contrast with FDR was instructive. Roosevelt had acted when international society was in deep disarray; Gorbachev acted because he understood that international society was historically triumphant.[15]

This appreciation of the new global setting took him to a place beyond the customary preoccupation of national leaders with power and wealth. One common reading of his stratagems was to see them as a botched attempt at enjoying the best of both worlds: revitalizing the economy to provide for both military and civilian needs and thereby resetting the competition with the United States at a higher level. This was the wary view initially adopted by higher-ups in the administration of George H. W. Bush who found it difficult to accept the possibility that Gorbachev would abandon the Russian tradition of power seeking unless forced to do so. And it continued to be the conviction of many Americans who, after the fact, were convinced that he had been strong-armed into capitulating because the United States held "the winning hand." For example, in explaining the collapse of the USSR, Bush's secretary of state James A. Baker III believed that "the Soviet leadership had concluded that they could no longer compete with the West, not economically and not militarily." But this was a superficial analysis, for Gorbachev was not compelled to act as he did by the pressures generated by American policies. On the contrary, his thinking went far beyond conventional power calculations.[16]

While tough-minded US cold warriors saw his reforms as a way of buying time for a resurgence of Soviet military might, Gorbachev understood that the trajectory of international society conflicted with a continuation of old-style geopolitics. As he put it, alongside the usual geopolitical jostling for position, "another trend, with equally objective causes, was gaining momentum—the process of the emergence of a mutually interrelated and integral world." This was a dangerous contradiction with serious consequences, for the old Soviet-style habit of thinking in term of east versus West had "placed the peoples of the Soviet Union in hostile opposition to most of the peoples of the world." Logically, but nevertheless astonishingly, he decided that accommodation to the new realities of globalization took priority over the pursuit of power. Hence his new foreign policy initiatives, or what he liked to call the "new thinking," sought to put the brakes on the arms race and to move beyond a system based on power politics, even to the point of taking some previously unthinkable measures of unilateral disarmament. Whereas the old thinking had pursued a foreign policy based on hostility, Gorbachev believed that peace demanded "movement towards globality and universality of civilization." The new thinking, commonly seen as making a virtue of necessity, was a well-reasoned derivation of Gorbachev's globalist understanding.[17]

The old way of dividing the globe into first, second, and third worlds, with the prospect of an eventual unification along socialist lines, no longer made sense because one world had already come into being. "The world economy is a single organism," Gorbachev told the United Nations General Assembly in 1988, "and no state, whatever its social system or economic status, can normally develop outside it." The only hope of success for socialism thus required working with globalization, not by operating against it. As if it were stealing a page from William Howard Taft's playbook, the party's Central Committee in 1985 spoke of "bringing international relations back into the channel of normal cooperation," that is, rejoining international society. Suggesting that policy makers had hitherto been ideologically oblivious to this epochal change in international society, his foreign policy adviser said of Gorbachev's approach: "this is a reunification of mankind on the basis of common sense." One way of defining culture is to see it as common sense, in this case a common sense that was presumably global.[18]

If sustaining a military rivalry was not at the heart of Gorbachev's new thinking, neither was the idea of economic competition. Even supposing that Gorbachev had wanted to match the affluence of the West, he acknowledged that achieving a comparable level of wealth lay well beyond the reach of his nation's system. True, he was aware of how miserably, relative to the West, the Soviet economy, archaic even by socialist standards, was performing, having witnessed firsthand the cornucopia of capitalist production. But he was no fan of consumerism, for the socialist ideal of sufficiency had nothing to do with the creation of a consumer society. Writing a decade after the collapse of the Soviet Union, he complained that "consumerism and the desire for things . . . have pushed into the background any desire for spiritual enrichment or cultural progress," though he failed to spell out how exactly socialism was better equipped to supply such a boon.[19]

All in all, the Soviet imperial-cum-ideological tradition was woefully ill adapted to deal with the globalized international environment. In this new world, to persist in power maneuvers would serve only to defend an out-of-date system that had no hope of displacing the global reality. Without drastic change, the Soviet Union was fated to be left behind, an increasingly irrelevant Cyclops of a nation in a world that had passed it by. But it was not simply Soviet behavior that was behind the times, for there was also a systemic problem. The geopolitics of the Cold War were obstructing powerful trends of a world that was "objectively united by the bonds of interdependence," which was giving rise to a new form of "international relations under which, one can no longer live under the ancient traditions of 'the law of the fist.'" By restructuring the old power-oriented politics of the world, a system that was based on coercion, the Soviet Union could make its own significant contribution to globalization by "launch[ing] the beginning of a world *perestroika*." Vladimir Putin, one of Gorbachev's reversionist successors, would later complain that "the demise of the Soviet Union was the greatest geopolitical catastrophe of the century," but for Gorbachev the old thinking that undergirded geopolitics was no longer a relevant frame of reference. The decisive consideration was, instead, global community. True, Gorbachev would continue to point out the shortcomings of the pure market model and insist on the universal appeal of socialist values, but these could only bear fruit historically, "on the other side of ideology," in a future to which the USSR would have little to contribute.[20]

As the USSR's influence contracted to the boundaries of a pan-Slavic empire, the Soviet-led "world" came apart at the seams. The collapse, when it came, was extraordinarily rapid. Within the space of a little more than two years following the surprise opening of the Berlin Wall in November 9, 1989, the communist regimes of the eastern bloc collapsed, mostly without violence (Romania being the exception). The aftermath was messy but not explosive, as many expected, for there was little danger of a global conflict. By the end of 1991, following some Byzantine internal politics, the Soviet Union had been dissolved, replaced by fifteen successor states around the perimeter of a new Russian federation. Had the Soviets deployed their tanks as ruthlessly as they had in 1953 in East Berlin, 1956 in Hungary, and 1968 in Czechoslovakia, the Cold War might well have continued, though in what form is impossible to say. But that does not obviate the fact that the erosion of the principal selling point of the Soviet system—its superiority as a system of production and distribution that catered to the deepest needs of human beings—had become an effete ideological product that could not be rejuvenated.

CULTURE CHANGE AS CONFLICT AND AS ACCULTURATION

None of this could have happened without an American foreign policy that midwifed the revival of international society and the leap into a second wave of globalization in the 1970s. In the nineteenth century, the assumption that globalization was unstoppable had left little room for political tampering with its mechanisms. In the Cold War, by contrast, the effect of US policy was to give global community the political nurture sufficient to reestablish itself and to flourish. The long stretch of time during which this commitment to globalization endured underscored the degree to which policy was addressed to long-range international trends as opposed to the ephemeral issues that dominate the headlines in democratic electoral cycles. The duration of that commitment was even longer when one factors in dollar diplomacy. From a longer perspective still, international politics had traveled a remarkable distance since the dawn of international relations.

That the Cold War had ended with a political victory for the United States could not have been clearer—after all, the nation's archenemy had suddenly passed away—but the causes of this success were extraordinarily muddled. As soon as it was over, a messy and inconclusive debate took place about who or what should take credit for the result. Depending on one's predilections, one could select from a baffling menu of options. I have chosen to emphasize Gorbachev's appreciation of changes in international society, but others have opted for Reagan's tough line and willingness to splurge on military modernization. Other possibilities include the contagious spread of the courage displayed by dissidents in eastern Europe, particularly in Poland and Czechoslovakia; heretical political leadership in the eastern bloc countries; the influence of the charismatic Polish pope, John Paul II; the relative failure of communism to provide a way of life as satisfying to most people as that generally available in the West; the computer revolution; American steadfastness over the entire forty-five-year life of the Cold War; *Ostpolitik*; the amazing spread of American popular culture; the role of nongovernmental organizations; the exposure of Soviet elites to life in the West; the example of China. One could expand the list still further. With history a picture puzzle that can be put together in many different ways, it is no wonder that historians have yet to provide a convincing causal explanation of this dramatic outcome.[21]

Assembled in this way, it is obvious that all these pieces of the puzzle have some merit and that no single explanation will do, for no one factor could have been effective in the absence of others—this mighty river was the product of many tributaries. Frustrating as it may be, this inability to explain precisely how and why things happened is typical of the way that historians wrestle with explanations of large-scale events. The more the historian focuses on broad phenomena like globalization, the more he is likely to lose touch with the small but certain cause and effect relationships that lend authority to historical studies that concentrate on more modest happenings. Historians inevitably lose sight of the complex connection between the parts and the whole as they climb up the rungs of generalization and abstraction by writing histories of histories—the higher the ladder, the more unsteady the explanation. Unlike natural science, history has no plausible procedure for uniting the macro and the micro in the way that physicists hope to bring together quantum mechanics and cosmology in a grand unified theory that comes close to explaining ultimate reality. Historians are perforce more modest. For those who appreciate its complexity, history is too vast and too tangled to explain in its totality. Historians cannot hope to gather enough evidence to accurately reconstruct it, and even then they would not be able to process it systematically. While parsimony is the holy grail of social scientific theory, simple historical explanations are for the simpleminded.[22]

If we want to understand how the Cold War ended, there is no way of extricating ourselves from a dense web of argumentation in which no single strand turns out to be the Ariadne's thread that leads the way out of the labyrinth. If we seek to account for the postwar world's distinctive political characteristics, the answers must be sought at least in part in ideology and culture, but changes in the ideational sphere cannot be explained without reference to the international economy, whose performance helped to generate, transmit, and sustain certain kinds of ideas. In turn, the international economy owed much to the political buttressing that had been retrofitted after the war. And, as we have seen, an explanation of victory and defeat in the Cold War is wholly inadequate without an understanding of how global culture has functioned. In short, globalized international relations cannot be convincingly construed in reductionist terms.

Despite this inherent complexity, one-size-fits-all political explanations have tended to command the limelight. The administration of George H. W. Bush received much well-deserved credit for bringing the Cold War to a "soft landing," thus breaking a historical pattern in which periods of dramatic change in the international system were marked by horrible crashes. But skillful pilots, though indispensable, explain only so much. Self-assured "nuclear abolitionists" like Ronald Reagan and Mikhail Gorbachev were important to ending the Cold War, but to attribute the outcome entirely to their military and foreign policies, their economic programs, their preoccupation with missile defense and the danger of nuclear war, and so on, is badly to misunderstand the historical process by which this outcome was reached. The Cold War could not have been ended without the diffuse transcultural understandings that operated outside of political reach. To continue with the aviation metaphor: even more necessary was a smooth and well-prepared runway, constructed over the course of a half century of generally successful globalization, which made possible a controlled touchdown. Had the landing taken place in mountainous or rocky terrain, the outcome would have been disastrous.

Training the spotlight on international society and on culture also puts the simplistic idea of Cold War victory in a new light. Though the Cold War ended in the triumph of one way of life over another, it was not a political conquest that liberal ideas "won." As one way of gauging the importance of international society, one might try to imagine the best case outcome (the worst case being a nuclear World War III) had international society been a nonfactor. In that case, as many historians of both left and right persuasions have suggested, there needn't have been a cold war at all because disagreements could have been put to rest by realistic deals of the "this is yours and that's ours" variety. A few American statesmen, Nixon and Kissinger, even agreed. Obviously, globalization has only a bit part to play in this kind of schema, which is what one might expect from explanations that are based on realistic political and military calculations. But the Cold War was not settled in this way because it would have required that the American foreign policy imaginary be drastically scaled back and altered beyond recognition. In the absence of this necessary background, constant wheeling and dealing of the Nixon-Kissinger variety would have been construed as appeasement, as they soon enough discovered.[23]

The other extreme option—force—also had its limits. The Cold War was not really a war because it could not be fought in the first place with purposive strategies, tactics, and weaponry designed to achieve victory. Though the Cold War was contested on many battlefronts, even at its most intense it may be more useful to think of it as a "hot peace." Even as a political description, the term "cold war" is a loaded expression that fails to capture the complexities of the relationship between the United States and the Soviet Union, which, as eventually came to be realized, was highly cooperative in many areas, sometimes in unspoken ways. By the 1980s, aside from some rhetorical fireworks, it had settled down, as a practical matter, into a live-and-let-live relationship. But if the Cold War was not a real war that could be fought or won, and if its ultimate outcome was dependent upon the workings of intercultural processes that could not be politically dictated, then it is questionable whether it makes sense to think of it as a power struggle. It may be that it is better understood as part a larger story about the evolution of international society and the spiky progression of the globalization process.[24]

As a fallback, one could resort to the competitive idioms of social Darwinism by recasting the Cold War as a cultural conflict. But such a move also has its difficulties. To be sure, there was an ideological and cultural front to the Cold War, where battle was joined quite seriously by officials who were tasked with waging and winning a struggle of ideas. The problem is that the metaphor of conflict or contest, which suggests much suffering, sacrifice, grief, and death, along with its connotation of clear-cut defeat or victory, does not fit a process that occurred insensibly outside the ambit of official foreign relations. There were wars, certainly, but important changes also took place in a quite unwarlike and mostly invisible fashion in the background that I discussed earlier, changes that could not be imposed or prevented by official means. "Defeat," rather than being dictated, took the form of a belated recognition by Gorbachev and his supporters of a historical metamorphosis that the apparatus of Soviet power was powerless to effectively oppose. For individuals behind the iron curtain, acknowledging the normality of a Western lifestyle was hardly a defeat. Nor was it a defeat for socialist societies in the aggregate, for whom the end of the Cold War, because it offered the opportunity for a better life, might more accurately be considered a victory for the supposed losers.

Bereavement is always a by-product of significant and rapid cultural change, but the conviction of die-hard communists that the outcome of the Cold War was a political debacle was every bit as misplaced as the Western belief in Cold War victory. For a struggle that was waged politically but resolved by global social and cultural processes, the non-coercive language of acculturation and cooperative cultural borrowing may be more appropriate than Darwinian metaphors. If the crucial developments took place on cultural ground, the view of the Cold War as a power struggle fails hopelessly to convey what was at stake, how the issues were resolved, and how gains and losses should be weighed. The claim that the United States did not win the Cold War as much as it was resolved in its favor is certainly arguable, and one's position depends on the degree to which one believes that the historical process can be shaped by foreign policy or any other use of instrumental rationality. As totalitarian societies have demonstrated, the scope of political control is enormous, but it was the ungovernable growth and intensification of international society and the emergence of an incipient global culture that made possible what power could not achieve.

So while American policy did play a significant role in the outcome, there was no political blueprint for cultural transformation on a global scale of the kind that occurred during the Cold War. It was not possible to predict beforehand, to plan for, or to manage the wave of Americanization and consumerism that washed over the world; nor was it possible to forecast the accompanying globalization of American culture, the degree of dependence upon foreign resources, and the impact on the American labor force and wages that would result from the pursuit of an open global economy. If it is the case that cultural innovations are conditioned by one's cultural inheritance, the presence of an embryonic global culture suggested that a widespread predisposition to welcome such changes was already in place—something that policy makers could not know ahead of time nor take advantage of. Just as evolution is a process of creation without a Creator, history is a play without a playwright.

Perhaps the wisdom of the crowd (which can at times be quite stupid) has something to tell us about the validity of the war metaphor. Take, for example, the flat popular reception accorded to the news that the Cold War had ended. Given the enormous amount of ideological PR with which the public had been carpet bombed for more than a generation, Americans took surprisingly little satisfaction in their historic achievement. Though many intellectuals indulged in triumphalism, there was no spontaneous outpouring of mass euphoria, relief, dancing in the streets, or victory parades of the kind seen, say, at the end of the Second World War. Unlike the conclusion of that conflict, the end of the Cold War did not feel like an earthshaking success. It was not a hollow victory, but neither was it rousingly fulfilling—many sports fans derived greater joy from the triumph of their favorite teams. This is hardly conclusive evidence, but it does suggest that the end of the Cold War was a world-historical event to which applying the word "victory," a political term with zero-sum connotations, is wholly inappropriate. So in answer to the question, "who won the Cold War?" I say, "global society."

The reason why victory felt so joyless had much to do with the new form taken by international relations during the Cold War. Until the nineteenth century, politics was thought to be the most important realm of human activity and the centerpiece of social knowledge. Until the middle of the twentieth century, Americans had thrown in their lot with international society. In the Cold War, politics returned to take up residence in a newly receptive American milieu, but it could not resume its once dominant place. It could not displace international society from the foreign policy agenda, and it had to stand by as culture took on an essential role in deciding the outcome of international issues. This transit from the political to the social and then to the cultural encompassed a complicated pattern of interactions to which the old political vocabulary of war, peace, domination, and subordination cannot do justice. Looked at in this way, much of the world's history in the twentieth century was a prolonged stretch of turbulence in the continued evolution of international society.

After seventy-five years of self-sequestration under Bolshevik rule, the collapse of the Soviet Union marked Russia's return to the civilizational fold. But Russia was not alone in experiencing a homecoming. For the United States, the Cold War had been a major departure from the course charted at the turn of the twentieth century. With international society apparently secure, the United States, like Cincinnatus, was in a position to return to its earlier more modest station in international affairs. On the other hand, the extraordinary power that it had amassed between World War II and the end of the Cold War made it possible for the United States to exercise a kind of hegemony that was quite new in world history.

Notes

1. Victoria de Grazia, *Irresistible Empire: America's Advance through Twentieth-Century Europe* (Cambridge: Belknap, 2005), 113–14. It would be unfair not to note that liberalism is no more enlightening when it comes to drawing the contours of the ideal society.
2. "Elite Theory," in *Blackwell Dictionary of Modern Social Thought*, ed. William Outhwaite (Malden, MA: Blackwell, 2003), 195.
3. Bill Keller, "Russia's Restless Youth," *NYT*, July 26, 1987, 27; Flora Lewis, "Oh, For a Normal Country," *NYT*, October 12, 1988, A31; Flora Lewis, "Watershed for Gorbachev," *NYT*, July 5, 1989, A21; Robin Finn, "Fetisov and Starikov, of New Jersey, U.S.A.," *NYT*, October 11, 1989, D30; Tom Malinowski, "Poland Settles Down to Democracy," *NYT*, December 8, 1990, L25; Flora Lewis, "After Five Years," *NYT*, December 12, 1990, A23. Yale Richmond, "Cultural Exchange and the Cold War: How the West Won," speech at the Aleksanteri Institute's Ninth Annual Conference "Cold War Interactions Reconsidered," October 2009, 29–31, University of Helsinki, Finland. From time to time, people in other countries have expressed a desire to live in "a normal country," e.g., Germany and Japan, post-Soviet Russia, Israel, Italy, and even the United States. The common thread here, I would argue, is the ability of international society to estrange people from national peculiarities that otherwise would remain culturally embedded.
4. Mark Twain, *Collected Tales, Sketches, Speeches and Essays*, vol. 2, *1891–1910* (New York: Library of America, 1992), 942; Peter Singer, *Hegel: A Very Short Introduction* (New York: Oxford University Press, 2001), 38. The continuing hostility of socialism to consumerism is evident in this response by President Evo Morales to an interviewer's question about how best to end capitalism: "It's changing economic policies, ending luxury, consumerism. It's ending the

struggle to—or this searching for living better. Living better is to exploit human beings. It's plundering natural resources. It's egoism and individualism. Therefore, in those promises of capitalism, there is no solidarity or complementarity. There's no reciprocity. So that's why we're trying to think about other ways of living lives and living well, not living better. Not living better. Living better is always at someone else's expense. Living better is at the expense of destroying the environment." See http://endofcapitalism.com/category/consumerism/.

5. Adam Smith, *The Theory of Moral Sentiments* (Minneapolis: Filiquarian Publishing, 1977 [1759]), especially chap. 3, 77. "Of the Corruption of our Moral Sentiments . . ." in which he argues, in a disapproving Presbyterian manner, that "it is from our disposition to admire, and consequently to imitate, the rich and the great, that they are enabled to set, or to lead what is called the fashion. Their dress is the fashionable dress; the language of their conversation, the fashionable style; their air and deportment, the fashionable behaviour. Even their vices and follies are fashionable; and the greater part of men are proud to imitate and resemble them in the very qualities which dishonour and degrade them."

6. The Olympic games featured all sorts of themes—among them nationalism, internationalism, Cold War conflict, and blatant commercialism—but the desire for host countries to be included, as well as for the international community to welcome them, is apparent from the selection of post–World War II sites for the summer games.

7. "China's President Lashes Out at Western Culture," *NYT*, January 4, 2012, A7.

8. Niall Ferguson and Moritz Schularick, *NYT*, November 16, 2009. A joke making the rounds was that the United States was obligated by treaty to come to the defense of Taiwan in the event of hostilities with China, but that it would have to borrow money from China to pay for it.

9. Manuel Castells, *The Information Age: Economy, Society and Culture*, vol. 3, *End of Millennium* (Malden, MA: Blackwell, 2010), 5–67.

10. Robert Service, "The Next Russian Revolution?," *NYT*, December 23, 1991. For arguments about the role of consumerism as a force in East Germany, see Susan E. Reid, "Cold War in the Kitchen: Gender and the De-Stalinization of Consumer Taste in the Soviet Union under Khrushchev," *Slavic Review* 61, no. 2 (Summer, 2002): 211–52.

11. Richard Nixon, "A War about Peace: The Victory of Freedom," *Vital Speeches of the Day* 57, no. 12 (April 1, 1991): 357.

12. Thomas Risse-Kappen, "Ideas Do Not Float Freely: Transnational Coalitions, Domestic Structures, and the End of the Cold War," *International Organization* 48, no. 2 (Spring 1994): 185–214; Emily Rosenberg, "Consumer Capitalism and the End of the Cold War," in *Cambridge History of the Cold War*, ed. Melvyn Leffler and Odd Arne Westad (New York: Cambridge University Press, 2010), 508–9. Gorbachev was, in my estimation, a greater and more imaginative leader than Woodrow Wilson. While both were able to penetrate beyond everyday happenings to an understanding of the deeper meaning of events, Gorbachev was able to question his belief system, something that the proud Wilson was incapable of doing.

13. *NYT*, January 6, 1987. On the role of fundamental vs. operative ideologies, see Martin Seliger, *Ideology and Politics* (New York: Free Press, 1976) and *The Marxist Conception of Ideology* (New York: Cambridge University Press, 1977), 4–5.

14. Zdenek Mlynar, *Conversations with Gorbachev* (New York: Columbia University Press, 2002), 153.

15. Gorbachev, *On My Country and the World* (New York: Columbia University Press, 2000), 175; Gorbachev, "A Common European Home," speech to the Council of Europe, Strasbourg, July 6, 1989, *Vital Speeches* 55, no. 23 (September 15, 1989): 706. Vladislav M. Zubok, *A Failed Empire: The Soviet Union in the Cold War from Stalin to Gorbachev* (Chapel Hill: University of North Carolina Press, 2007), 303–35; Gorbachev Nobel lecture, June 15, 1991.

16. James Baker, *Spiegel* interview, September 23, 2009, Spiegel Online International.

17. Gorbachev, *On My Country and the World*, 39; Gorbachev Nobel lecture, June 15, 1991.

18. Gorbachev, *On My Country and the World*, 181; Vladislav M. Zubok, "New Evidence on the End of the Cold War," *Cold War International History Project Bulletin*, no. 12/13 (Fall/Winter 2001): 13; Clifford Geertz, "Common Sense as a Cultural System," *Local Knowledge*: *Further Essays in Interpretive Anthropology* (New York: Basic Books, 1983), 73–93.

19. Robert D. English, *Russia and the Idea of the West: Gorbachev, Intellectuals, and the End of the Cold War* (New York: Columbia University Press, 2000), 40; Matthew Evangelista, *Unarmed Forces: The Transnational Movement to End the Cold War* (Ithaca, NY: Cornell University Press, 1999); Mikhail Gorbachev, *On My Country and the World*, 269.

20. Mikhail Gorbachev, "International Affairs, Asia and the Pacific Region," July 28, 1986, *Vital Speeches of the Day* 52, no. 23 (September 15, 1986): 707; Andrei Grachev, *Gorbachev's Gamble: Soviet Foreign Policy and the End of the Cold War* (Cambridge, MA: Polity, 2008), 233. Gorbachev's rough treatment of the Baltic states may appear to contradict this assertion. I prefer to see it as a tactical deviation.

21. Obviously, I have no sympathy for the view that Ronald Reagan deserves chief credit for ending the Cold War, which is a parochial and simpleminded view of history.

22. One can, at least in principle, imagine a time when complex historical problems will be tackled by large teams of historians, not unlike the hundreds of scientists who collaborate in particle physics. I doubt that this will ever come to pass, and if it ever does, I doubt that the histories produced by such collaboration will amount to much.

23. Those who argue that realistic deal making would have spared the world much agony tend to neglect a very important feature of realist thinking, viz., that deals are not made for their own sake. They are expressions of the limitations placed upon states by power realities. But because, in the realist scheme of things, the state system is based on the pursuit of power, such deals are by their very nature only temporary. Hence instability and insecurity are destined to reemerge in more menacing form as states ratchet up their power potentials.

24. Thomas Paterson, *On Every Front: The Making and Unmaking of the Cold War* (New York: W. W. Norton, 1992), 230, maintains that "the Cold War actually had no winners. Both the United States and the Soviet Union had spent themselves into weakened conditions and were in a state of decline and collapse." This accords with Gorbachev's view that "we all lost the cold war." But this way of looking at things still frames the outcome in terms of winners and losers.

Questions for Reflection

In these Perspectives excerpts, the authors deal with some of the critical turning points in the story of the West. Despite the allied victory in WWII and the hunger for peace that followed, these selections remind us that postwar life was still about battles: some on the home front and some in hot spots of superpower conflict and ambition. As you reflect on the meaning of such encounters, then and now, answer the following questions.

1. How and why did the PTA become a Cold War battlefront in the United States? Describe some of the activities to prevent communist influence.

2. How did men view these activities? According to the excerpt, what was the wider impact of this campaign? Brennan writes that "Women became key players in the evolution of the Right." Based on this excerpt, do you agree?

3. The second excerpt deals with Operation Ajax. What was that? Who was Kim Roosevelt?

4. Wilford writes that "Orientalist attitudes clouded his [Kim Roosevelt's] judgment of Persian politics." What does he mean? How did this attitude lead to seeing Iran as a playground for spies?

5. In the third excerpt, what explanations have been given for the decline and fall of communism?

6. Ninkovich's answer to "Who won the Cold War?" is global society. What does he mean?

7. How do the examples above demonstrate the influence of ideology?

8. In your view, which of the examples above best demonstrates the post-WWII definition of power? Which excerpt to you is most persuasive?

Activities Menu
Your instructor may assign one or more of the following learning activities:

Prewriting Exercise
Take a minute and write a paragraph (half page of notebook paper) on what you know about the impact of the Cold War at home in the U.S.

Media
Select a relevant video program from one of the following and write a one-page (double-spaced) reaction.

- TED Talk
- Munk Debates
- C-SPAN
- Crash Course

Source Search
Select and read two related primary sources found online at the Modern History Sourcebook and incorporate them into your essay.

Short Essay I
Write a three-page (double-spaced) essay of about 750 words in answer to the following question: Drawing on the material from this chapter, discuss the role of American women in the anticommunist campaign during the Cold War.

Short Essay II

Write a three-page (double-spaced) essay of about 750 words in answer to the following thesis. Defend or refute: "Operation Ajax is a classic case of American imperialism."

Role-Playing Exercise: Developing a Persuasive Argument

Divide the class into three or four teams and debate the reasons for the collapse of communism, both in Eastern Europe in 1989 and in the Soviet Union at end of 1991.

Suggested Reading

Mary Brennan, "Women Arise: The Red Threat on the Domestic Scene," in *Wives, Mothers, and the Red Menace: Conservative Women and the Crusade against Communism* (2008)

Hugh Wilford, "Authoring a Coup, 1953," in *America's Great Game: The CIA's Secret Arabists and the Shaping of the Modern Middle East* (2013)

Frank Ninkovich, "Americanization, Globalization, and the End of the Cold War," in *The Global Republic: America's Inadvertent Rise to World Power* (2014)

Allan M. Winkler, *The Cold War: A History in Documents* (2011)

Vladislav M. Zubok, *A Failed Empire: The Soviet Union in the Cold War from Stalin to Gorbachev* (2008)

Chapter 8

Chapter Skill	Doing Digital Research
Chapter Issue	Violence & the Body Politic
Chapter Objectives (Students will...)	• Identify three specific ways in which violence affects the body politic • Assess one perspective on violence and the body politic • Demonstrate in a discussion the ability to work with digital historical materials
Assignments and Assessments	1. Read the Setup Narrative 2. Listen to the Lecture(s) 3. Read the Perspectives excerpt 4. Take part in a role-playing Class Discussion 5. Take the Final Exam

Setup Narrative: Violence & the Body Politic

Violence is the scourge of our time. It besets every corner of the globe—and in a digital age, we can't avoid it. Every day we wake to more stories of terror, senseless shootings, and vindictive politics, and we seem to be enthralled with entertaining ourselves this way, too. This is nothing new to the post-9/11 world. In 1968, a day after Martin Luther King, Jr., was assassinated, and just two months before his own death at the hand of an assassin, Robert Kennedy gave a remarkable speech that rings with relevance nearly 50 years later.

In 1944, picturesque Bretton Woods, New Hampshire was the setting for an international finance conference that proved to be a turning point. Some 44 nations came together and agreed on a postwar economic order that included new institutions like the World Bank and the International Monetary Fund, both capitalized at billions of dollars to help with postwar recovery. A few years later, the Marshall Plan distributed 13 billion to do the same, and the growth of allied economies at seven and eight percent indicated that money and institutions were doing some good. At home in the U.S., the gross national product increased from 227 billion to 488 billion in the two decades after 1940. Wages rose 30% and median family income nearly doubled. Inflation remained at a flat, manageable 1.5% throughout much of the 1950s.

The Marshall Plan gave a needed boost to our trading partners, while the G.I. Bill offered countless vets—and the country at large—an increase in productivity to the world's leading economy. The American middle class grew as did American corporations. All the while, labor unions were strong and the tax code favored the growing middle class. The greatest generation had survived the Great Depression and the recent world war, and they could look with cautious confidence on the future of their children.

But their children had other ideas. Many who had been raised in the prosperous postwar economic recovery believed they saw their elders settle for a faceless, mindless, and heartless setup: a company job, a home, two kids, and a predictable round of social engagements and expectations, all of which became an imperative rather than a choice. At the same time, they looked around the world and saw multiple injustices and multiple platforms of protest that demanded not just a new politics but a new lifestyle as well, one that was now accompanied by a fresh, upbeat soundtrack of the times. The postwar era rocked and rolled with movements ranging from decolonization to civil rights and gender to sexual orientation rights. Yes, prosperity we had, but the wrongs of social powerlessness and racial, gender, and sexual discrimination had to be righted. Those movements often had a life cycle of their own, and as we look closer at the Civil Rights Movement, its phases offer insights into the postwar world and its bent toward militancy.

Returning black war veterans became veterans of desegregation, and they piloted the movement into a period of legal victories that included cases like Brown v. Board of Education (1954). Between 1960 and 1964, legislative and moral victories captured the imagination of the country, and Martin Luther King's dream found practical expression in the Civil Rights Acts of 1964 and the Voting Rights Act of 1965. The years 1965 to 1968 witnessed the exacting turmoil of implementing legislative gains on streets and in neighborhoods, as well as the spreading controversy of the U.S. involvement in the Vietnam civil war that we call the Vietnam War. In a single year, 1968, we lost two prominent spokesmen for progressive change, Martin Luther King, Jr., in April and Robert Kennedy in June; experienced the most contentious national political convention in our history; and looked around the world and realized that peoples from Mexico City to Tokyo were dealing with many of the same things we were.

Fragmentation in the Civil Rights Movement reflected a rise in protest and organizational militancy, and groups like the Weather Underground and the Black Panthers took their own paths to defining postwar America. Beyond the borders of the U.S., in Western and global contexts, these organizations reflect broader discontent with an increasingly globalized, elite-rewarding superstructure that led powerless citizens to believe they had no recourse to anything but rage against the system—and the body politic suffered for it. So did our reputation abroad as countries from Nicaragua to Iran saw a cavernous and abiding hypocrisy in American rhetoric as U.S. foreign policy consistently propped up dictators in the name of fighting communism. Meanwhile, in Muslim majority countries, fundamentalist schools of thought gave birth to radical splinter bands that, we realized after 9/11, could weaponize modern technology for their ends. Historically speaking, they sought to overcome the legacies of Western imperialism by a Muslim revival expressed in a new caliphate, but one established by force of arms and raids with a militancy and ferocity not seen in centuries.

And yet the hue and cry of violence is not just "over there." School shootings, police brutality, revenge politics, and sophomoric religious mores are part of our body politic. The digital age and the truth have an uneasy relationship—it's a reflection of who we are. When did the loyal opposition in American politics become an enemy to be vanquished in blood sport? When and how did our neighborhood streets become war zones? Is it the arsenal of guns that characterizes American culture and entertainment? Is it because of the influence of money? Big questions for a single chapter to be sure, but ones we cannot fail to ask—and answer. Listen to what Robert Kennedy had to say in a speech given the day after Martin Luther King, Jr., was assassinated.

Lecture

Pay attention to the chapter lecture(s), either online or in class.

Tips on Doing Digital Research

+ Thank those who did the work! Imagine the time it took to scan, digitize, and design what you see on a fine digital history site. Be grateful you don't have to travel halfway around the world to get to a source or cache of resources.

+ Remember that just because it's on the web doesn't make it so. Remember the issues with the print revolution in Chapter 1? Same here, probably more so.

+ Watch those dot-coms. They're not evil (at least most of them), they're just put together in different ways and for different reasons than .edu or .org sites. Look for sites with standard supporting information, references, and apparatus. And look for those noted in other reputable publications.

+ Focus. A single page on a single site can take time to sort out, so please do yourself a favor: focus.

+ Cite properly. Be sure to give credit where credit is due (normally the url and the date retrieved). And don't even think of plagiarizing. It's a bad habit and, if not broken, it can cost you your job and reputation.

Remarks to the Cleveland City Club, April 5, 1968

by Robert F. Kennedy

Cleveland City Club

April 5, 1968

This is a time of shame and sorrow. It is not a day for politics. I have saved this one opportunity to speak briefly to you about this mindless menace of violence in America which again stains our land and every one of our lives.

It is not the concern of any one race. The victims of the violence are black and white, rich and poor, young and old, famous and unknown. They are, most important of all, human beings whom other human beings loved and needed. No one—no matter where he lives or what he does—can be certain who will suffer from some senseless act of bloodshed. And yet it goes on and on.

Why? What has violence ever accomplished? What has it ever created? No martyr's cause has ever been stilled by his assassin's bullet.

No wrongs have ever been righted by riots and civil disorders. A sniper is only a coward, not a hero; and an uncontrolled, uncontrollable mob is only the voice of madness, not the voice of the people.

Whenever any American's life is taken by another American unnecessarily—whether it is done in the name of the law or in the defiance of law, by one man or a gang, in cold blood or in passion, in an attack of violence or in response to violence—whenever we tear at the fabric of life which another man has painfully and clumsily woven for himself and his children, the whole nation is degraded.

"Among free men," said Abraham Lincoln, "there can be no successful appeal from the ballot to the bullet; and those who take such appeal are sure to lose their cause and pay the costs."

Yet we seemingly tolerate a rising level of violence that ignores our common humanity and our claims to civilization alike. We calmly accept newspaper reports of civilian slaughter in far off lands. We glorify killing on movie and television screens and call it entertainment. We make it easy for men of all shades of sanity to acquire weapons and ammunition they desire.

Too often we honor swagger and bluster and the wielders of force; too often we excuse those who are willing to build their own lives on the shattered dreams of others. Some Americans who preach nonviolence abroad fail to practice it here at home. Some who accuse others of inciting riots have by their own conduct invited them.

Some looks for scapegoats, others look for conspiracies, but this much is clear; violence breeds violence, repression brings retaliation, and only a cleaning of our whole society can remove this sickness from our soul.

For there is another kind of violence, slower but just as deadly, destructive as the shot or the bomb in the night. This is the violence of institutions; indifference and inaction and slow decay.

Robert F. Kennedy, "Remarks to the Clevland City Club, April 5, 1968," *Robert F. Kennedy Senate Papers.* John F. Kennedy Presidential Library and Museum. 1968.

This is the violence that afflicts the poor, that poisons relations between men because their skin has different colors. This is a slow destruction of a child by hunger, and schools without books and homes without heat in the winter.

This is the breaking of a man's spirit by denying him the chance to stand as a father and as a man among other men. And this too afflicts us all. I have not come here to propose a set of specific remedies nor is there a single set. For a broad and adequate outline we know what must be done. When you teach a man to hate and fear his brother, when you teach that he is a lesser man because of his color or his beliefs or the policies he pursues, when you teach that those who differ from you threaten your freedom or your job or your family, then you also learn to confront others not as fellow citizens but as enemies—to be met not with cooperation but with conquest, to be subjugated and mastered.

We learn, at the last, to look at our brothers as aliens, men with whom we share a city, but not a community, men bound to us in common dwelling, but not in common effort. We learn to share only a common fear—only a common desire to retreat from each other—only a common impulse to meet disagreement with force. For all this there are no final answers.

Yet we know what we must do. It is to achieve true justice among our fellow citizens. The question is now what programs we should seek to enact. The question is whether we can find in our own midst and in our own hearts that leadership of human purpose that will recognize the terrible truths of our existence.

We must admit the vanity of our false distinctions among men and learn to find our own advancement in the search for the advancement of all. We must admit in ourselves that our own children's future cannot be built on the misfortunes of others. We must recognize that this short life can neither be ennobled nor enriched by hatred or revenge.

Our lives on this planet are too short and the work to be done too great to let this spirit flourish any longer in our land. Of course we cannot vanish it with a program, nor with a resolution.

But we can perhaps remember—even if only for a time—that those who live with us are our brothers, that they share with us the same short movement of life, that they seek—as we do—nothing but the chance to live out their lives in purpose and happiness, winning what satisfaction and fulfillment they can.

Surely this bond of common faith, this bond of common goal, can begin to teach us something. Surely we can learn, at least, to look at those around us as fellow men and surely we can begin to work a little harder to bind up the wounds among us and to become in our hearts brothers and countrymen once again.

Questions for Reflection

In this Perspectives excerpt, Robert Kennedy paints a vivid picture of the culture of violence in the modern West, in America especially. As you reflect on the impact of violence on our national life, then and now, answer the following questions.

1. What was the climate in the United States in the spring of 1968? What phases had the Civil Rights Movement gone through?

2. What quote by Lincoln does Kennedy include in his speech? Track down when and where Lincoln first said this.

3. According to Kennedy, what were the features of the culture of violence in 1968?

4. What does Kennedy mean by the "violence of institutions"?

5. What does Kennedy recommend to escape the cycle of violence? Be specific.

6. In your view, is this speech realistic or idealistic?

7. What connections can you make between the conditions in America in the spring of 1968 and the conditions in America today?

8. This excerpt can be found on the Internet, as can so much of our past now. In your opinion, what is the promise and peril of digital history?

Activities Menu

Your instructor may assign one or more of the following learning activities:

Prewriting Exercise

Take a minute and write a paragraph (half page of notebook paper) on what you know about Robert Kennedy.

Digital History

Research and select at least two examples of digital history: one good, one bad. Be prepared to discuss what you found.

Source Search

Select and read two related primary sources found online at the Modern History Sourcebook and incorporate them into your discussion.

Class Discussion I

Use the questions above as the basis of a class discussion about the impact of violence on the body politic. Be prepared to be called upon.

Class Discussion II

Use the questions above to talk about the parallels between America 1968 and America now. Are there similarities? If so, what are they? Can we overcome our culture of violence?

Role-Playing Exercise

Have members of the class assume the following roles: a mayor or other elected representative, a police officer, a community organizer, a religious leader, and residents of marginalized sections of your community. Hold a discussion so that each has a chance to answer the following: where do we go from here?

Final Exam
Complete a final exam created by your instructor.

Suggested Reading
www.jfklibrary.org

Martin Luther King, Jr. *Where do we go from here? Chaos or Community* (2010)

National Commission on Terrorist Attacks upon the United States: The 9/11 Commission Report (2004)

Martha C. Nussbaum, *The New Religious Intolerance: Overcoming the Politics of Fear in an Anxious Age* (2012)

Olivier Roy, *Holy Ignorance: When Religion and Culture Part Ways* (2009)

Bibliography

Benedict Anderson, *Imagined Communities* (1991)

Edward Ball, *Slaves in the Family* (1998)

David Blackbourn, *The Long Nineteenth Century: A History of Modern Germany, 1780–1918* (1998)

James Cracraft, *The Revolution of Peter the Great* (2003)

Jonathan Daly, *Historians Debate the Rise of the West* (2014)

John Dower, *Cultures of War: Pearl Harbor, Hiroshima, 9/11, Iraq* (2010)

Terry Eagleton, *Reason, Faith, and Revolution: Reflections on the God Debate* (2009)

Catherine Evtuhov, *The Cross & the Sickle: Sergei Bulgakov and the Fate of Russian Religious Philosophy, 1890–1920* (1997)

Niall Ferguson, *Civilization: The West and the Rest* (2011)

Johanna Fernández, ed., *Writing on the Wall: Selected Prison Writings of Mumia Abu-Jamal* (2015)

Alexander Herzen, *My Past and Thoughts* (2009)

Hajo Holborn, *The Political Collapse of Europe* (1951)

Steven Johnson, *How We Got to Now: Six Innovations that Made the Modern World* (2014)

George F. Kennan, *Sketches from a Life* (1989)

Martin Luther King, Jr., *Why We Can't Wait* (2000)

Lionel Kochan and John Keep, *The Making of Modern Russia* (1997)

Mahmood Mamdani, *Good Muslim, Bad Muslim: America, the Cold War, and the Roots of Terror* (2004)

Reinhold Niebuhr, *Moral Man and Immoral Society* (1932)

James Sheehan, *German History, 1770–1866* (1993)

Sam Wineburg, *Historical Thinking and Other Unnatural Acts: Charting the Future of Teaching the Past* (2001)

CPSIA information can be obtained
at www.ICGtesting.com
Printed in the USA
LVHW061904020621
689160LV00005B/8